SIMPLE
VEGETABLE
GROWING

SIMPLE
VEGETABLE
GROWING

Ian Walls

WARD LOCK LIMITED · LONDON

ACKNOWLEDGEMENTS

The publishers gratefully acknowledge the following agencies and company for granting permission to reproduce the following colour photographs: David Pople (pp. 11, 22 lower, 42 and 90); Suttons Seeds Ltd. (pp. 15, 19, 30, 34 and 70); Pat Brindley (pp. 22 upper, 35, 51 left, 71, 78, 83 and 87); and the Harry Smith Horticultural Photographic Collection (pp. 31, 51 right and 91). The photograph on the cover and on p. 2 was taken by Bob Challinor.

All the line drawings are by Nils Solberg.

Front cover: Mixed vegetables, courtesy Harry Smith Horticultural Photographic Collection.

First published in Great Britain in 1988
by Ward Lock Limited, 8 Clifford Street
London W1X 1RB, an Egmont Company

House editor Denis Ingram
Text set in Bembo by
Hourds Typographica, Stafford

Printed and bound in Portugal by
Resopal

British Library Cataloguing in Publication Data

Walls, Ian G.
  Simple vegetable growing. — (Concorde
    gardening).
    1. Vegetables
    I. Title   II. Series
    635   SB322

    ISBN 0-7063-6624-7

Frontispiece: A neat, well-kept vegetable plot can fit happily in the flower-filled surroundings of a country cottage garden.

CONTENTS

PREFACE

No-one could claim that vegetables are difficult to obtain at your local greengrocer's or supermarket. The supply of vegetables is now a year-round international affair, with produce from far and wide, especially during the winter. But the quality of what you buy varies greatly, as does the price. It only needs a cold snap in the winter for the price of leeks or cabbages to soar. Many of the vegetables you buy can look nice, but the important thing is their flavour. There is just nothing to equal freshly picked or pulled produce straight from the garden. What is more, you can grow the varieties *you* want and like.

Growing vegetables requires a little time and effort, it is true, as they don't grow by themselves. But it is rewarding and not difficult. This little book explains in simple down-to-earth terms exactly how to achieve maximum success.

I.G.W.

CHAPTER I

PLANNING FOR VEGETABLES

MAKING A CHOICE

Vegetables differ in the way they grow in different regions, different soils and different gardens, so you often need to compromise between what you want to grow and what you *can* grow. On the practical side, can you cope with the work involved? This varies a lot between different types of vegetables: potatoes, for example, are a lot more labour-demanding than a few lettuces or cabbages.

Table 1 shows the main range of vegetables you are likely to want to grow, with some notes about soils, region, the amount of work involved and main cropping period. To start with run down the list and make your selection. We can then move to the next stage – planning production in more detail.

Table 1. Vegetable Planner

Crop	Ease of growing and work involved	Soil type	Region	Main cropping period
Asparagus	Much work in preparing beds and raising plants. Weed control can be a problem.	Medium, light peaty.	Does best in warmer areas.	Mid-late spring.
Beans				
Broad	Not demanding.	All soils.	Very hardy everywhere.	Mid-summer until autumn. Freeze well
Dwarf French	Not demanding.	All soils.	Best in warm areas. Excellent under cloches.	Late summer into autumn. Freezes really well.
Runner	Support means work.	All soils.	Best in warm areas.	Late summer into autumn. Freezes.

Crop	Ease of growing and work involved	Soil type	Region	Main cropping period
Beetroot	Not demanding.	All soils.	Everywhere. Good under cloches for early crop.	Stores well.
Broccoli (see cauliflower)				
Brussels sprouts	Not demanding.	All soils.	All areas.	Autumn/ spring. Freezes too.
Cabbage	Not demanding, apart from preventive measures against cabbage fly and caterpillars.	All soils.	Everywhere.	Available over long period. Summer through to spring if there is a good choice of varieties and types.
Carrot	Can be tricky due to carrot fly. Needs regular weeding.	All kinds, but best in light soils.	All areas. Early crops under protection.	Superb crop – when you want it over a long period. Stores well.
Cauliflower/ Broccoli	Not demanding.	All soils.	Winter broccoli best in warm areas. Not so productive in the North.	Grow different varieties to get good succession from mid-summer onwards. Freezes well.
Celery self-blanching and ordinary	An easy crop to grow.	All soils, but likes light or peaty land.	All regions but loves cloche protection to start with.	From mid-summer onwards. Freezes too.
Cucumber	Fairly easy but needs constant watering.	All soils but likes good local preparation.	Warmth-loving. Best in frames or greenhouses except in warm regions.	Mid-summer into mid-autumn in warm areas.

Crop	Ease of growing and work involved	Soil type	Region	Main cropping period
Endive	Like lettuce, an easy crop.	All soils.	All regions.	Autumn through winter, depending on climate.
Gourds	Fairly easy.	Well-drained soil.	Warm corners.	Late summer into autumn.
Herbs	Most quite simple.	All soils.	All regions.	Available over a long period. Always useful.
Kale	Easy.	All soils.	All regions.	All winter until mid-spring.
Leeks	Easy to grow but require attention.	Rich soil only.	All regions.	Over very long period.
Lettuce	Simple	All soils	All regions. Early and late crops need protection; winter crops good light and heating.	With successional cropping, over very long period according to district.
Marrow/ Courgettes	A bit demanding, especially watering.	Rich soils or compost.	All regions.	Mid-summer until weather spoils them.
Mustard & Cress	Easy to grow.	All soils.	All areas. Winter cropping under protection.	Over long period if sown regularly in right conditions.
Onions	Easy, especially spring onions and onion sets.	All rich soils.	All areas.	Spring onions from late spring; bulb onions from late summer; all winter from storage.

Crop	Ease of growing and work involved	Soil type	Region	Main cropping period
Parsley	Easy, but carrot fly and rust disease are problems.	All soils.	All areas, but protection required for winter.	Over long period according to weather. Can be protected in winter.
Parsnip	Easy.	All soils.	All areas.	From early autumn over long period.
Peas	Easy	All soils	All regions. Early crops under cloches.	From early summer into autumn, but freeze superbly.
Potatoes	Easy, though planting and lifting can be hard work.	All soils.	All areas.	From early/mid-summer onwards as they store well.
Radish	Easy	All soils.	All regions. Early crop under protection.	From late spring onwards.
Rhubarb	Simple to grow. Some forcing techniques are demanding.	All soils.	All areas.	From early/late spring well into autumn, but gets a little tough.
Shallots	Simple.	All soils.	All regions.	From late summer, but stores well like onions.
Spinach	Easy	All soils.	All areas.	Over long period according to type and variety.
Sweet Corn	Fairly easy.	All soils.	Likes warmth to mature.	From early/late summer, but

Crop	Ease of growing and work involved	Soil type	Region	Main cropping period
Sweet Corn (continued)			Must be started under glass in cold areas.	freezes really well.
Tomatoes	Demanding.	Rich soil.	Warm areas only for outdoor crops. Greenhouse for best results.	Under glass or protection from early summer to mid-autumn. Results variable outdoors.
Turnips and Swedes	Easy but clubroot troublesome.	All soils.	All areas.	Autumn to spring.

Frequent hoeing destroys weeds at the seedling stage and prevents surface soil becoming compacted and airless.

PRODUCTION STRATEGY

When you have decided what vegetables you would *like* to grow and, more important, stand a reasonable chance of growing well, the next stage is to decide *where* to grow them. Then you must get the land ready to receive them. This takes time, patience and physical effort – plus some essential tools for the work.

TOOLS FOR PRODUCING FOOD ON SMALL SCALE

(Figs. 1–3)

Riddle
Trowel and dibber
Fork
Hosepipe on reel
Garden line, reel and pins
Watering can
Wheelbarrow
Digging fork
Digging spade
Border spade
Shovel
Draw hoe

Dutch hoe
Metal rake
Cultivator/crumbler
Wooden hay rake
Straight boards
Flame gun, small sprayer
Hand precision seeder
(Rotary cultivator or small tractor for larger scale production, which can be hired)
Sprinkler for watering

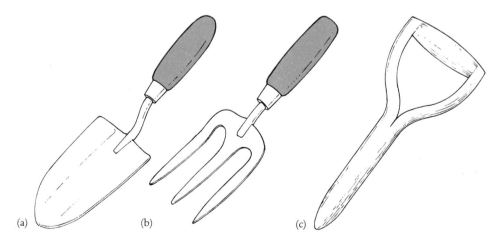

(a)   (b)   (c)

Fig. 1 (*a*) A hand trowel for planting; (*b*) a hand fork for weeding; and (*c*) a dibber for planting seedlings, are essential tools.

Fig. 2 (*a*) A spade for digging and (*b*) a digging fork for loosening and breaking up ground. Both must be of the right size and a smaller border fork (*c*) is very popular with ladies.

LOCAL CLIMATE

There are considerable local variations on regional climates, so every gardener must assess his own situation carefully. The slope of his plot, and of different areas on it, greatly affects the amount of sun and warmth it absorbs. North-sloping land is colder and later than south-sloping land in northern latitudes; the converse is true in the Southern hemisphere. Hills deflecting wind and precipitating rain make one garden totally different from another just a mile away. Since cold air sinks, a garden in a hollow is likely to suffer more severely from frost than the regional average. Seek advice from your local garden centre, or better still, your local horticultural society, which is bound to include a lot of experienced gardeners.

Fig. 3 (*a*) A draw hoe for ridging or taking out seed or planting drills; (*b*) a dutch hoe for surface weeding; and cultivators, (*c*) and (*d*), of different sizes should be part of every gardener's essential equipment.

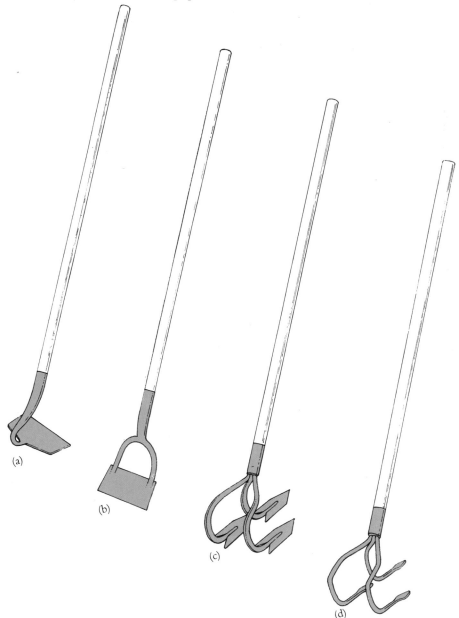

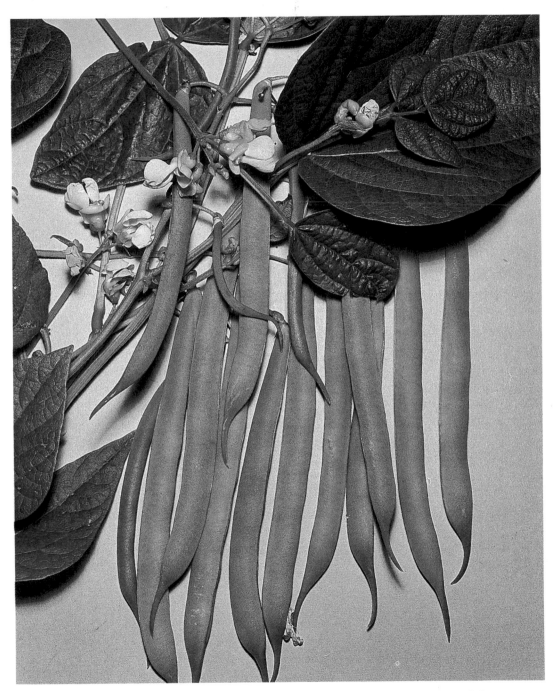

Dwarf French beans like 'The Prince' form tender pods to be eaten young or left to ripen and yield haricots.

CHAPTER 2

SOIL PREPARATION

CROP ROTATION

The first thing to appreciate is that most vegetables (and some short-term fruits such as strawberries) should be moved around the garden to avoid growing them repeatedly in the same spot, which gives rise to pest, disease and nutritional problems. This is really common sense. For example, if you grow cabbages in the same spot year after year clubroot (Fig. 4) can build up in the soil to a crippling level. But grow them just one year and you may have only a trace of clubroot. If you move them on and give the ground a rest from crops susceptible to clubroot (all brassicas), when cabbages are again grown on that spot clubroot is no longer a

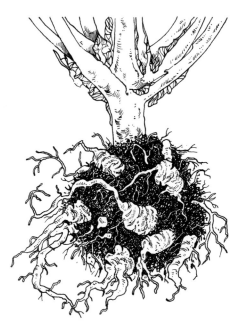

Fig. 4 Club root disease results in swollen, evil-smelling roots of brassicas.

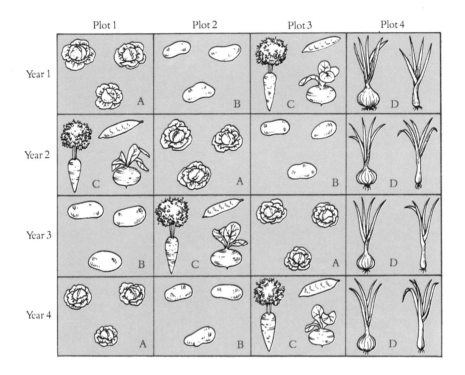

Fig. 5 Crop rotation is an important part of vegetable growing and should be carried out systematically. A = Brassicas; B = Potatoes; C = Roots & legumes; D = 'Permanent' crops.

serious hazard. Some plants exude their own particular acid or 'body scent', which can build up to a 'sickness' if they are grown year after year in the same place. Cabbages also take quite a bit of nitrogen out of the soil, so it makes sense to move them to freshly manured land and follow them with crops which do not like so much nitrogen, such as peas and beans, and carrots and beetroot, which can fork or distort badly in freshly manured soil.

Crop rotation is highly desirable then, if not essential, for many aspects of continual crop production. It is necessary now to work out an acceptable way of practising it.

It is usual to run a three-year rotation, involving three beds of more or less equal size. A fourth area can be made into a semi-permanent bed for onions, leeks and asparagus. The most commonly practised rotation is shown in Fig. 5, but there are several variations.

Plot A
Brassicas, including cabbages, cauliflowers, kale, savoys and sprouts, intercropped with lettuces or other small salad plants. Note that these are all surface-growing crops.

Treatment
Use farmyard manure or compost. Lime the ground during the winter and give general fertilizer at 70–140 g per m² (2–4 oz per sq yd) before planting or sowing. During the season the only extra feeding required is liquid feeding, or a side dressing (a pinch or scatter of fertilizer alongside the crop) of Nitro-chalk or some other quick form of nitrogen.

Plot B
Potatoes, both early and maincrop. The early types can be followed by broccoli and in some districts by spring cabbages. Leeks can also follow early potatoes.

Treatment
Use farmyard manure or compost. No lime is given unless a soil test indicates that it is needed. Use a general fertilizer at 70–140 g per m² (2–4 oz per sq yd) before planting potatoes and any crops which follow.

Plot C
Root crops and legumes, including carrots, parsnips, turnips, beetroot, peas, beans, spinach. Lettuces can also be grown on this plot.

Treatment
Farmyard manure or too much compost is *not* used except for preparing pea and bean trenches. Use a good general fertilizer at 70–140 g per m² (2–4 oz per sq yd) before sowing or planting.

Plot D ('permanent')
The onion plot, also leeks, asparagus, etc.

Treatment
Liberal amounts of farmyard manure or compost used along with general fertilizer at 70–140 g per m² (2–4 oz per sq yd) before sowing or planting.

It is reasonably simple to set one part of a standard allotment aside for permanent crops and divide the remainder into three equal beds. But few modern gardens offer this kind of space, or if they do it is rarely in a neat rectangular plot. However, beds separated by paths, though not so easy to work, have the advantage of some protection from the spread of pests and diseases. Make a rough plan of your garden and decide on the sites of your four beds. There is nothing wrong with vegetables intermixed with flowers, especially flowers for cutting such as dahlias or chrysanthemums, though it goes against the grain to turn a lawn, rockery or rose bed into a potato or cabbage patch.

As its name implies, the early-cropping beetroot 'Boltardy' is unlikely to run up to flower to the detriment of the crop.

CHECKING ON PESTS AND DISEASES

With a new garden, try to find out how the land was previously used. If it was under permanent turf for a long while you will be able to grow crops for years with little bother. If it was cultivated, try if possible to find out if there was any trouble from clubroot of brassicas or potato cyst eelworm. You could have the soil checked for its eelworm cyst content – something a keen grower should certainly do.

Large pests like wireworms and leatherjackets can be seen when digging and can be dealt with during cropping (see also Appendix, p.93–94).

WATERING FACILITIES

In some areas and some seasons there is enough natural rainwater to sustain outdoor crops. This is especially so in the North (UK). In other areas unless extra watering can be supplied the crops will fail. Under glass or polythene protection all water must be supplied artificially. So it is essential to provide a sufficient supply of water for the scale of production, and the equipment to apply it. In an average suburban garden a standpipe, hose and sprinkler are the basic needs.

PLANNED CROPPING

Remember that sowing moderate quantities of quick-maturing crops in succession gives supplies over a period and avoids a wasteful glut of vegetables. This applies especially to lettuces, radishes and spinach. There are obviously limits to the number of successional sowings that can be made, since summer lettuces sown after mid-summer for example, cannot be expected to mature successfully out of doors. But the succession can be extended by using early-, mid- and late-maturing varieties of vegetable, which should be borne in mind when planning cropping.

Traditionally the food-producing garden has always been set apart from the decorative garden. But if space is restricted one might have to break with tradition. Remember, however, to leave room for a compost heap.

CLEARING WEEDS
(SEE APPENDIX)

The intensive cultivation of some vegetables such as potatoes can have a profound clearing effect on weedy land. In general though it is far better to deal firmly with the weeds before starting intensive cultivation, and long enough before cropping for the weedkilling chemical, if any, to be dissipated.

Sodium chlorate is frequently used for cleaning land before cropping. But remember that it is dangerous and inflammable stuff, especially when it has dried on foliage. Paraquat/diquat weedkillers, on the other hand, are good for cleaning things up, and leave no nasty residues about, merely killing off surface growth.

Land infested with couch grass can be cleaned up with dalapon following the directions given with the product and strictly observing the interval that must elapse before cropping.

KEEPING RECORDS AND CROPPING TIMETABLES

It is well worth taking the time and trouble to keep records of sowing and planting dates, yields and any serious problems encountered. A few notes on varieties are helpful as memories are all too short and such information can easily be forgotten by the time the next batch of seeds needs to be ordered.

ORGANIC GARDENING

This is assuming considerable importance these days and it means ideally not using any form of artificial inorganic chemical for growing crops or making composts. Many gardeners compromise by using chemical compost makers. Gardeners interested in the whole sphere of organic gardening are advised to get in touch with The Soil Association, 86–88 Colston Road, Bristol, Avon, BS1 5BB (0272-29066). The Soil Association can give advice on all aspects of organic gardening and the addresses of other bodies who can help gardeners interested in organic growing. The main bodies are: Henry Doubleday Research Association, Ryton-on-Dunsmore, Coventry, CV8 3LG (Tel: 0203 303517); and Scottish Organic Gardener, Brigton Gardens Cottage, Douglastown by Forfar, Angus, DD8 1TL.

DEALING WITH WEEDS, PESTS AND DISEASES AND USING CHEMICALS

Readers are advised, when considering using any chemicals in the garden to control weeds, pests or diseases, to obtain a copy of the directory of garden chemicals produced annually by the British Agrochemicals Association Ltd., 4 Lincoln Court, Peterborough, PE1 2RP (tel. 0733 49225). Gardeners preferring organic methods are reminded that flame guns, mulching with various materials or black polythene mulch are key weed control techniques. Organic gardeners should also realise that a longer rotation than normal is advised to deal with many soil borne pests and diseases. An up-to-date directory of chemicals is given in the Appendix.

Formerly a hardy midwinter vegetable, Brussels sprouts now have a greatly extended season and have become very popular.

Summer cabbages with distinctive pointed hearts provide a welcome change from the so often repeated salads.

CHAPTER 3

SITE SELECTION AND USE

BEST PLACES TO GROW VEGETABLES

Siting a vegetable bed in sun or shade, or in rows north to south, or east to west, can speed or slow down the rate of maturing. North or south allows a more even entry of sunlight, though in a south*-facing bed in front of a wall the run matters little. Intercropping saves time and space – quicker maturing vegetables are grown between slower growing ones, eg. lettuces between beans. Catch cropping is also useful – this is growing a quick crop on a temporarily vacant site, eg. radishes on the side of prepared celery beds.

SHELTER

Shelter is important, especially in an exposed area. It can be provided by hedges, which some gardeners do not like because they rob the soil of food and moisture and create heavy shade. They need cutting too! Artificial shelter can be readily provided by wattle or interwoven fencing, but be sure to set it firmly in the ground in concrete or it could easily be blown over. Netting materials are becoming very popular and do not create shade.

THE USE OF GREENHOUSES/POLYTHENE STRUCTURES, FRAMES AND CLOCHES FOR VEGETABLES

Details of greenhouses can be found in *Simple Greenhouse Gardening* (edited by Alan Toogood, Ward Lock) or more comprehensively in *The Complete Book of the Greenhouse* (Ian Walls, Ward Lock). Figs. 6 and 7 show a garden frame and cloches respectively. Using these various forms of protection for vegetable growing can extend productivity considerably for the keen gardener. A heated greenhouse, especially if equipped with a propagating case, is invaluable for raising early plants.

* *North*-facing in Southern Hemisphere

THE IMPORTANCE OF HARDENING OFF

All plants raised under glass or other protection must be gradually weaned to outdoor conditions by giving progressively more ventilation, or putting them outdoors on warmer days and bringing them back under cover if there is any risk of frost. Taking plants straight out of a greenhouse and expecting them to thrive outdoors is foolhardy. It pays to be cautious.

COMPOSTS FOR RAISING AND GROWING PLANTS

Sowing vegetable seeds and planting outdoors demands the use of seed-

Fig. 6 A cold frame is excellent for raising a wide variety of plants, especially if it is of the taller type with ventilators provided, as here.

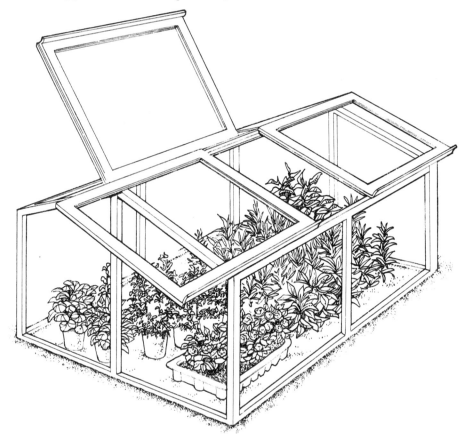

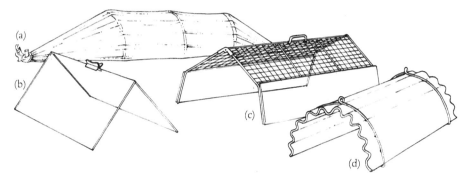

Fig. 7 Cloches or polythene tunnels have an important role for vegetable growing. See them at your local garden centre.

sowing and potting composts. The same is true for plants grown to maturity in pots or growing bags, like tomatoes, cucumbers and some other crops.

There are still two basic types of compost: soil-based following the John Innes formula, and those which are peat-based. Peat-based composts have become very popular in recent years, largely because they are so convenient, being easier to mix without any need to sterilise the basic ingredients. Both types of compost can be bought at any garden centre. Select seed composts for seed sowing and potting composts for growing on. For those wishing to mix their own, the following are useful basic formulae:

JOHN INNES SOIL-BASED COMPOSTS

A bushel is equivalent to a box 55 × 55 × 25 cm (22 × 10 × 10 in)
A 9 litre (2 gallon) bucket = $\frac{1}{4}$ bushel (9 litres)
One bushel = 36 litres
Peat is now sold in litres

FOR SEED SOWING

2 parts (by bulk) loam (good soil), ideally sterilized
1 part (by bulk) peat (good quality, good texture)
1 part (by bulk) sharp sand or fine gravel

To each bushel (36 litres) of this mix, allowing for 15–20% shrinkage, add:
42 g (1$\frac{1}{2}$ oz) superphosphates and
21 g ($\frac{3}{4}$ oz) ground limestone
or a proprietary slow-release fertilizer such as Vitax Q4, Chempak (*no* lime needed), or Osmocote according to directions. Perlite can be used in place of sand at recommended rates.

Fig. 9 (*a*) For seed sowing use a garden line to mark your drills; (*b*) take out a shallow drill with the edge of a draw hoe; (*c*) sow seeds thinly; and (*d*) cover up firmly and rake level.

lumps. The ground is then made suitable for sowing by treading and raking. A little experience goes a long way with regard to these practical operations.

MECHANICAL CULTIVATION

More and more gardeners now use rotary cultivators or small ploughs to cultivate soil. While nothing can beat careful digging a hired or bought machine can be very quick and effective.

HOEING AND TAKING OUT SEED DRILLS

This also is best explained diagrammatically. Hoeing for weed control is reasonably simple and involves moving the hoe to and fro near the surface. To take out seed drills, lay down the garden line, make it taut and use the corner of a draw hoe or other type of hoe to take out a shallow cavity, about 1.5–2.5 cm ($\frac{1}{2}$–1in) deep. Having sown the seeds, refill the cavity, firm with the feet and then rake over (Fig. 9).

Deeper drills, for sowing peas or beans are made in much the same way.

SEED SOWING INDOORS AND OUT

A seed is a miniature resting plant wrapped in a protective coat. The three requirements to trigger off growth are air, moisture and suitable temperature. It is important therefore to sow indoors, or outside when conditions are right. Sowing in cold, wet soil outdoors is generally a waste of good seeds as they simply rot because it is too cold for them to germinate. The same can be true if they are sown too deeply in wet soil. Conversely, seeds sown in light sandy soil too near the surface can dry out.

The important thing with indoor sowing is to avoid wasting seeds. There are three basic methods:

1 Sow seeds broadcast, very thinly in open trays (Fig. 10). Then prick out the little seedlings while young into either other trays giving them more space (Fig. 11), or in little pots. The plants are then grown on and gradually acclimatized for planting out of doors.

2 If the seeds are large enough to handle individually, sow them directly

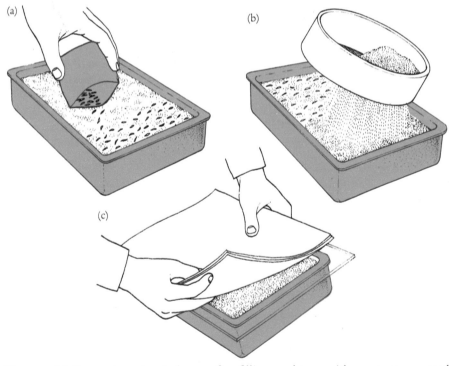

Fig. 10 (*a*) For seed sowing indoors, after filling seed tray with compost sow seed thinly; (*b*) cover seed lightly with compost using a fine riddle; (*c*) cover with a sheet of paper and glass and place in warmth to germinate. Covers must be removed *as soon as seeds germinate.*

Suitable varieties of cauliflowers are hardy enough to allow us the pleasure of this delectable vegetable during the dark winter months.

in cell trays (Fig. 12) or open trays by pushing the seeds lightly into the surface. If given enough space at the outset, the seedlings can be left until large enough and hardened off for planting out of doors.

3 Many seeds are now sown directly in pots (Fig. 13) or soil blocks. The ease with which this can be accomplished again depends on the size of the seed. Once the seeds have germinated, the plants are grown on and eventually planted out after hardening off.

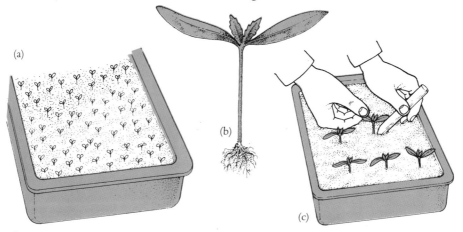

Fig. 11 (*a*) Seedlings showing through compost; (*b*) seedling ready for transplanting; (*c*) seedlings are inserted into potting compost (pricked out), where they are grown on slowly ready for planting out.

Many gardeners and gourmets consider the celery which needs blanching greatly superior to the self-blanching type.

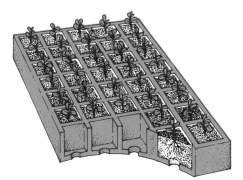

Fig. 12 Showing construction of a polystyrene cellular tray. These trays are most useful where the seeds are large enough to handle individually.

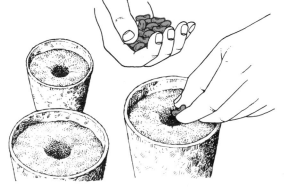

Fig. 13 Large seeds can also be sown directly into various types of individual pots or containers.

TRANSPLANTING

Transplant from pots or boxes into the open ground only when conditions are suitable for planting out. Use a trowel or dibber to take out a suitable planting hole. Set the plant in this with the least possible root disturbance, firm it gently (Fig. 14) and water it in. Continue watering if the weather is exceptionally dry, until the plant is established.

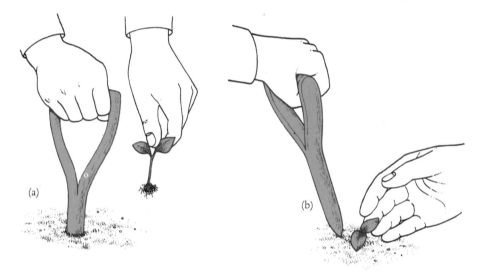

Fig. 14 Planting seedlings out with dibber. Note that the seedlings should be held gently by their leaves, never by their stems. Watering in helps their establishment.

MULCHING

This is becoming an important technique, especially popular with organic gardeners. Apart from peat, garden compost or shredded bark, it can be done with black polythene or materials such as Hortopaper, which breaks down eventually to supply valuable organic matter.

IMPROVING AND FERTILIZING THE SOIL

PLANT FOODS

All growing plants need essential elements to enable them to grow. These are called plant foods. The major elements are nitrogen (N), phosphate (P_2O_5), potassium (K), calcium (Ca), magnesium and sulphur. Elements essential in smaller amounts, called trace or micro-elements, include iron, boron, manganese, copper, zinc and molybdenum. Sodium and chlorine are also now thought to be essential.

The gardener has to consider two distinct aspects of soil fertility:
1. Soil structure or physical texture – a matter of the size of its mineral particles and amount of organic matter (popularly called humus) it contains. A good structure is essential for plant roots to be able to breathe.
2. The quantities and balance of essential major and trace elements present in the soil *actually available* to the plants.

The acidity or alkalinity, called pH, which is a measure of lime (calcium) content, is also critical.

Feeling and looking at a soil help assess its texture whereas soil analysis in a laboratory or with a testing kit is needed to find out the pH and whether the soil is well supplied with the necessary elements. (See Index Factors, p.35).

BULKY ORGANIC MATERIALS AND ORGANIC GROWING

Bulky organics such as farmyard manure supply amounts of the main elements (ie nitrogen, phosphorus and potassium) along with trace elements. They are most useful for improving the physical condition of the soil. Composts contain the full range of plant nutrients.

FERTILIZERS AND MANURES

Table 2 (p.34) shows the relative speed of action and nitrogen/phosphate/potash content of some of the most commonly used fertilizers.

GREEN MANURING

This is an old practice which should never be overlooked as a means of improving soil structure. It includes growing a quick crop such as rape, vetches, annual lupins or mustard thickly on bare ground and then digging, forking or rotovating it in *before* it flowers.

Italian ryegrass can also be used to great effect, sown at about 18 g per m² (½ oz per sq yd) in the autumn or in the spring and turned in before it flowers, along with some nitrogen. Its virtue lies in the mass of root fibres it leaves in the ground, plus the value of the straw.

COMPOUND FERTILIZERS AND LIQUID FOODS

Many different types of proprietary compound fertilizer, including liquid

Table 2. Fertilizers and manures

Fertilizer/Manure	Action	Nitrogen (%)	Phosphate (%)	Potash (%)
Basic slag	Slow	15		
Bone meal	Slow	5	20	
Dried blood	Medium	10		
Farmyard manure	Slow	0.5	0.25	0.5
Fish meal	Quick	10	8	7
Guano	Quick	15	10	7
Kainit	Slow			13
Nitrate of soda	Quick	16		
Nitro-chalk	Quick	16		
Potassium nitrate	Quick	14		
Poultry manure	Medium	3	2	6
Rape meal	Slow	5	2	1
Seaweed	Slow	5		1.5
Shoddy (wool)	Slow	12		
Sulphate of ammonia	Quick	20		
Sulphate of potash	Medium			50
Superphosphate	Medium		15	
Used hops	Slow	4	2	

fertilizers, are marketed. Analysis is often given on the packet as a percentage ratio of the main nutrients N, P, K, always in that order, eg 7:7:7; 10:7:10; 6:10:18. This convention has been followed in the cultural notes as a guide to main nutrient needs, *but ratios are not critical*. To use these fertilizers effectively, measure the area to be treated, weigh out the

Ridge cucumbers, grown in the open vegetable plot, are an undemanding crop yet yield prolifically.

Kale 'Tall Green Curled' is very hardy and a valuable source of winter greenstuff, besides being attractive in appearance.

correct quantity and apply it evenly, by hand from a bucket or through a properly set fertilizer distributor. Follow directions given with the product and do not over-apply. It is vital to follow the recommended dilution rate for liquid fertilizers. Applying too early in the season can be wasteful as some can be leached from the soil. Applying too late could damage the crops.

INDEX FACTORS

These are included in the cropping notes as a simple guide to soil fertility.

Nitrogen	Index 1–2	average fertility
	Index 3	high fertility
Phosphate	Index 1–2	low fertility
	Index 2–3	average fertility
	Index 4–5	high fertility
Potash	Index 1–2	low fertility
	Index 2–3	average fertility
	Index 4–5	high fertility

CHAPTER 5

SELECTION OF EASY TO GROW VEGETABLES

ASPARAGUS

Hardy. Has been grown for several hundreds of years as a luxury vegetable and today canned asparagus tips are much in vogue. *Asparagus officinalis* produces separate male and female plants. The former are more productive and therefore selected for cropping.

Site and soil preparation Likes well-drained soil in a warm area. pH 5.5–6. Soil index N:P:K 2–3. Deep digging is essential when preparing beds, as asparagus has very deep, searching, spreading roots. Also, asparagus beds will be down for 10–30 years. Put in farmyard manure at 9–11 kg per m² (20–25 lb per sq yd) during digging, when the soil should preferably (though not essential) be built up into beds a metre or more wide. At planting time fork in a complete balanced fertilizer 10:7:10 at 70 g per m² (2 oz per sq yd) plus a light dressing of 18 g per m² ($\frac{1}{2}$ oz per sq yd) bonemeal close to the roots.

Each year after this mulch with well-rotted farmyard manure, applied with general fertilizer 7:7:10 in early spring. Agricultural salt could also be added at 35–70 g per m²/1–2 oz per sq yd at the same season.

Sowing and planting Seeds required: 28 g (1 oz) per 30 m (100 ft) row. Viability 70 per cent.

Asparagus can easily be raised from seeds sown in mild heat in early spring or outdoors in mid to late spring. In early spring sow seeds in boxes (24 per box) and lightly cover with riddled soil. Outdoors sow in drills 5 cm (2 in) deep, 30 cm (1 ft) apart, or similarly in frames. When large enough, set out young plants 30–38 cm (12–15 in) apart and leave for two years until they flower. Mark the non-berried male plants with coloured raffia or by other means. Alternatively buy in male plants.

Plant in mid-spring in trenches 15–17 cm (6–7 in) deep and 30–45 cm (12–18in) apart. It is usual to have three rows to one raised bed. Current commercial practice is to plant in rows 1.2–1.5 m (4–5 ft) apart and there is some virtue in this method for easy management in the garden. Set the plants carefully on the bottom of the trench on a ridge of soil with a scattering of bonemeal, and merely cover the roots with soil until the plants are seen to be growing. Then complete filling the trench. Do not allow crowns to dry out while planting.

General cultivation Lightly fork over the beds in mid-spring and hand-weed or hoe. Simazine can be used before growth emerges, paraquat/diquat to clean up beds in spring, and dalapon (against couch grass) for crops grown in established beds. Prevent drying out, especially of young beds. Some root restriction may be necessary when the asparagus starts to wander from older beds, and this is best done with a sharp spade. Some support may be required in summer. In autumn, cut off the yellow foliage very carefully to avoid damaging the shoots. In winter earth up with soil from between rows. Though beds can have a life of as much as 30 years, in practice ten years is long enough, due to the cluttered growth and weeds which develop.

Harvesting and storing Cut stalks with a sharp knife about 8 cm (3 in) beneath the surface when the tips are seen to be breaking the soil surface. Stop cutting by early summer. Will store only in freezer.

Pests and diseases. Look out for asparagus rust, which turns the leaves a rusty brown – use a range of fungicides. Violet root rot – plants will wilt and die; scrap beds and start with new stock in a new position. Asparagus beetle – red beetles with black heads and larvae eating shoots. Spray with Gamma-HCH, Derris (Rotenone) or Derris/Carbaryl in early summer.
Plants per person 10   *Yield per plant* 0.7 kg (1½ lb)

Varieties Giant Mammoth, Martha Washington, Perfection, Connover's Colossal (early).

BEANS, BROAD
Hardy. There are three types: 1. Magazan or fan-podded, i.e. dwarf with small pods containing an average of three seeds. Not generally grown today as they have a small yield compared with other types. 2. Longpod – with long pods as the name suggests, containing numerous seeds. Suitable for autumn or spring sowing. They take up a lot of room and should not be crowded into a small space at the risk of disease. 3. Broad pod – the best winter type, with short flat pods containing large seeds which can be white or green.

Site and soil preparation Any soil, preferably heavy, but good drainage essential. pH 6.5–7, soil index N:P:K 2–3. There is a risk of wind and frost damage in exposed situations, especially when autumn sown.

The trench method of growing them has many advantages. Take out trenches 30–45 cm (12–18 in) deep and fill to within 15 cm (6 in) of the top with well-rotted farmyard manure or compost and leave to settle. If convenient, you could take out the trenches in the autumn and fill them with garden waste as it becomes available, provided time is given for the ground to settle. Failing this, dig deeply and work in some farmyard manure or compost at 5–6 kg per m² (10–12 lb per sq yd).

If farmyard manure is dug in or the trench method is used, merely apply low nitrogen fertilizer 6:12:18 at 70 g per m² (2 oz per sq yd). (Beans are legumes and extract nitrogen from the atmosphere). Super-phosphate and sulphate of potash each at 35 g per m² (1 oz per sq yd) would be advisable if you cannot obtain a low nitrogen general fertilizer. If farmyard manure or compost is not available use fertilizer 6:9:18 at a heavier rate, 210 g per m² (6 oz per sq yd). Fish-derived fertilizer is much used commercially because of its organic origin.

Sowing and planting Seeds required 400 g (14 oz) per 30 m (100 ft) row. Viability 70 per cent.

There are several ways of sowing broad beans. The most usual is to take out a flat-bottomed trench 12.5 cm (5 in) wide and 5–7.5 cm (2–3 in) deep, with a draw hoe along a garden line, after applying fertilizer. Space the seeds 12–15 cm (5–6 in) apart in a double staggered line. Alternatively sow in a single drill 5–7.5 cm (2–3 in) deep taken out with a hoe, and set the seeds 12–15 cm (5–6 in) apart. Space rows 75–120 cm (2 ft 6 in – 4 ft) apart.

Sow Magazan or Longpod in mid-autumn in mild areas or in late winter/early spring. Use cloches to protect autumn or early spring sowings. In very cold districts beans can be sown in peat pots under glass for planting out in mid-spring. Beans can also be sown in peat pots in cold frames in the autumn and transplanted in spring.

Residual type weedkillers are used commercially, but the home gardener will find paraquat/diquat weedkiller used 5–7 days after sowing, but *before* emergence, is better. Hoeing with a *small* hoe, coupled with hand weeding, is not difficult on a moderate scale.

General cultivation Hoeing, hand-weeding and support are the main requirements, especially the latter in exposed areas. Support by erecting 1–1.5 m (4–5 ft) double stakes 1–1.5 m (4–5 ft) apart with strong string between them, or wire netting in a double row, using a wide enough mesh to allow for easy handling. A little extra feeding will be required, using a quick-acting source of nitrogen or a liquid feed. Pinch out the tops of the plants at the first signs of blackfly, cleanly removing the top.

Harvesting and storage Harvest over a period when beans are ready and still soft. (Open a few pods to inspect them.) Clear ground as soon as beans are harvested to avoid needlessly using up plant foods in the soil. Will store only by deep freezing, which is suitable only for young beans.

Plants per person 5   *Yield per plant* 113–226 g (4–8 oz)

Pests and diseases Look out for blackfly – aphids congregating on tips of shoots. Pinch these out and spray with insecticide. Bean beetles and weevils biting holes in leaves – spray with Gamma-HCH or Malathion at flowering stage. Leaf spots – control not usually necessary. Chocolate spot – attacks pods but does not usually harm seeds. If concerned, spray with Benlate or Bordeaux mixture. Grey mould, usually encouraged by damp weather, can also be troublesome, rotting seeds in the ground before germination. Buy treated seeds or treat them with seed dressing *before* sowing.

Varieties Aquadulce (autumn sown); Threefold White (good for freezing); Imperial Green Longpod, Imperial White Longpod (extra long pods); Giant Four Seeded White Windsor, Giant Four Seeded Green Windsor; Giant Exhibition Longpod, Masterpiece Green Longpod. Many others available, including special types.

BEANS, FRENCH

Both dwarf and climbing types are available, including varieties suitable for growing under glass. French beans are not related to broad beans. They are tender annuals that will not stand frost. The green pods are eaten whole, or the ripe seeds dried as haricot beans.

Site and soil preparation Warmer, lighter types of soil, well drained. pH 6–7, soil index N:P:K 3. A good, sunny, sheltered situation is essential for successful cultivation, especially for climbing beans. Failure with French beans is common in a poor summer or exposed situation, but much can be done to overcome climatic difficulties with cloches or by raising the plants under cover. Always choose a suitable variety for the region concerned.

Deep digging needed. Manure as for broad beans. Use a low nitrogen fertilizer 4:6:9 at 140 g per m² (4 oz per sq yd).

Sowing and planting Seeds required: 400 g (1 pt) per 30 m (100 ft) row. Viability 80 per cent.

Sow as for broad beans, but not until mid/late spring as they are very susceptible to frost. More widely spaced single rows are generally desirable for climbing types. A thiram-based seed dressing is always advisable as a routine treatment to prevent damping off. Where cloches are used, place them over the ground a week or so before sowing. Seeds can be sown singly in 5 cm, (2 in) peat pots for planting out later.

General cultivation Similar to broad beans, but take great care to avoid drying out. Climbing beans are usually supported with nylon or string netting on stout 2.5 m (8 ft) long poles, pushed about 60 cm (2 ft) into the ground. Paraquat/diquat is best used as a pre-emergent weedkiller in home gardens.

Harvesting and storing Use pods when young. Preserve in salt or use for deep freezing.
Plants per person 5   *Yield per plant* 56–112 g (2–4 oz)

Pests and diseases Slugs – use bait. Blackfly – spray regularly with insecticide. Flower dropping – mulch soil and avoid excess dryness.

Varieties Dwarf: Masterpiece; The Prince (both flat podded); Sprite (round podded and stringless; good for freezing), Canadian Wonder (maincrop), Loch Ness (upright), rounded stringless pods), Tendergreen (round fleshy pods, stringless, suitable for freezing), Blue Lake (climbing, stringless).

BEANS, RUNNER
Half-hardy. Runner beans need a warm climate if they are to grow well. In colder areas choose only favoured or sheltered situations. Even a successful crop will depend on the type of summer.

Site and soil preparation Most soils suit runner beans, but light, well-drained ones are more productive. pH 6–7, soil index N:P:K 2–3. Shelter from strong prevailing wind is essential, especially on a small scale where there is not the shelter provided by the beans being grown en masse.
  Apply fertilizer 10:6:12 at 40 g per m² (4 oz per sq yd) before sowing. It is most beneficial to take out a trench before sowing and fill it with compost to within 15 cm (6 in) of the surface.

Sowing and planting Seeds required: 400 g (1 pt) per 12–15 m (40–50 ft) double row or 24–50 m (80–100 ft) single row. Viability 75 per cent.
  Sow out of doors from late spring in the South and early summer in the North. Earlier crops are possible by sowing in peat pots in a cool

greenhouse three weeks before planting out. Avoid sowing too early because of the rapid growth which some varieties make under glass. Successional sowings can be practical until early summer but not much later. Sow seeds 15–20 cm (6–8 in) apart and 5–8 cm (2–3 in) deep in single rows. For double rows take out 5–7 cm (2–3 in) drills, and sow 25–30 cm (10–12 in) apart. Runner beans take up a lot of room, so leave plenty of space – 1.8–2 m (6–7 ft) or more – between rows. Alternatively, firmly fix 2.4–3 m (8–10 ft) bean poles 90 cm (3 ft) apart in the ground in tripod form giving a climbing height of about 180 cm (6 ft), 30–35 cm (12–14 in) apart. Sow two beans at the base of each pole, later discarding the weaker seedling.

General cultivation Runner beans must be supported from the outset, tying in the young plants, if not with bean poles then with string netting set on stout poles to give a height of at least 1.8m (6 ft), strong enough to stand the heavy weight of fully laden plants. Hoe as necessary and water in very dry weather. Spray water on to the flowers in dry weather to help them set. Pinching the plants when some 45 cm (18 in) high and again when at the tops of the supports will produce bushier plants.

Weedkillers as for French beans.

Harvesting and storing Pick regularly, taking young and succulent beans. Preserve in salt or use young in deep freeze.

Pests and diseases Slugs – use bait. Blackfly – spray regularly with insecticide. Flower dropping – mulch soil and avoid excessive dryness.

Varieties Enorma (for the exhibitor); Achievement (freezes well); Streamline; White Emergo; Kelvedon Marvel (grows over the ground without support); Crusader (for the exhibitor).

Beans of other types
The Haricot, a type of French bean grown for its white seeds, is the most popular. Also excellent for cooking whole. Grow as French beans, a good climate being necessary to ripen them. Asparagus beans have cylindrical green pods up to 60 cm (24 in) long and are grown like runner beans. Flageolet beans are green-seeded French beans, grown like them. Lima beans, the butter beans bought in shops, require warmth to grow well and rarely succeed in northern areas. They are grown like runner beans. Soya beans, valued for their distinctive oily flavour, are grown like dwarf French beans. They need warmth.

Plants per person 10   *Yield per plant* Nearly 1 kilo (2 lb)

Leeks, like 'Musselburgh' here, with their mild onion flavour are a great standby for digging as required in winter.

Pests and diseases Aphids, red spider, anthracnose, foot rot, mosaic virus, botrytis, rust, sclerotinia, flower dropping, bacterial blight, halo blight.

Varieties Most firms have their own specialities.

BEETROOT

Half-hardy. Probably originally a European native. There are two main types, Globe and Long, named after the shapes of the roots. There are also spinach and seakale beet, grown for their stalks and leaves as substitutes for seakale and spinach. They are grown very much like ordinary beet. For general purposes globe beetroot is more satisfactory to grow than the long type, and easier to cook whole.

Site and soil preparation Beet will grow in most soils but will develop the best shape and quality in soil which has *not* received fresh farmyard manure, which can produce forking and coarse woody flesh in the beet. Good manuring the previous year at fairly heavy rates gives the land a good texture. Aim at pH 6. Soil index N:P:K 2–3. Choose a sunny but not exposed situation.

Deep digging is necessary. Cultivation should be thorough and the soil raked down to a good tilth and well consolidated to ensure good, even seed germination and continuous uninterrupted growth. Long beetroot must have very well-cultivated and well-prepared soil. Fertilizer 6–8:6:12 should be applied before sowing at 140 g per m² (4 oz per sq yd), evenly spread or concentrated in the seed-drill area.

Sowing and planting Seeds required: 28 g (1 oz) per 15 m (50 ft) drill. Viability 60 per cent.

Young, newly germinated beet will stand no frost at all, as it causes them to run to seed. Therefore do not sow until all risk of frost is past – from mid to late spring, according to region. Successional sowings can be made until early summer for young roots for salads. Cloches or tunnels can be used to grow earlier crops and earlier sowings can also be made in a greenhouse. Sow seeds thinly in drills 1.5 cm (½ in) deep and 30 cm (1 ft) apart, remembering that an ordinary beet seed is in fact a cluster of seeds. Rubbed beet seeds, including monogerm, also sown very thinly. For small 'pulling' beet aim to have early seedlings 5–8 cm (2–3 in) apart. Big beet should be 15–20 cm (6–8 in) apart. Space spinach beet and sea-kale as long beet.

If necessary use paraquat/diquat a day or so before or after sowing.

General cultivation Apart from inter-row hoeing – take care to avoid nicking the beet – and thinning out, little is required as beet are a relatively straightforward crop to grow. After thinning, a light top dressing of nitrate of potash, or even common salt, helps to encourage growth and improves the quality of the roots. Watering may be necessary in dry weather.

Harvesting and storing Pull young summer beet when ready, and not too large, and twist off the leaves. For salads or for cooking as a vegetable they are best young. Lift mature crops carefully in autumn and twist off the leaves. (Cutting off leaves can cause bleeding.) Mature beet can be stored in a dry, frost-proof, dark shed, in boxes of sand or peat, or in a properly made clamp outside. Beet are often boiled and bottled in vinegar. Small beet can also be deep frozen.

Cut seakale and spinach beet leaves and stalks as needed. The leaves can be used in salads when very young, or treated as spinach. The thick white stems can be tied in small bundles and cooked separately. Any flowers which appear may be cooked as sprouting broccoli.

Plants per person 48   *Yield per plant* Up to 225 g (8 oz) depending on type

Pests and diseases Blackfly and aphids – spray regularly with a range of insecticides. Flea beetles biting holes out of leaves – dust with Gamma-HCH. Scab – scars on beetroot, not generally too harmful, usually caused by too much lime in the soil. Various fungi and mildews, along with leaf spots – spray with fungicides if these occur at a time of year when they are likely to be damaging. Damping off disease, when seedlings die, usually as a result of sowing too early in cold soil.

Varieties Boltardy (for early crop); Detroit Globe (for later use and storing during winter); Perpetual or Spinach Beet (leaves can be cut all season); Avonearly (early, resists bolting); Cylindra (quality and colour of Detroit; will slice with little waste); Imperial Early Globe (deep coloured flesh, practically non-bleeding); Bikores (early, high quality, deep coloured globe).

BORECOLE See Kale

BROCCOLI, SPROUTING; CALABRESE
Half-hardy. Frequently classed with cauliflower, but multi-hearting as opposed to single-headed. Calabrese, or green-sprouting broccoli, has become extremely popular in recent years.

Site and soil preparation Grows well in most types of soil, except the very lightest, where failure is common due to drying out. pH 6–7, soil index N:P:K 2–3. Any reasonable situation will do.

Ground should be well but not over-cultivated, as broccoli like firm land, particularly land that has been under turf for many years and only recently broken. When newly broken turf is used, or the previous crop was well dressed with organic manures, no farmyard manure is necessary. Otherwise dig in farmyard manure or compost at 5 kg per m² (10–12 lb per sq yd). Give a high potash fertilizer 4:6:12 at 140 g per m² (4 oz per sq yd) before sowing or planting. There is no need for a superlative finish to the soil, especially when planting rather than sowing direct.

Sowing and planting Seeds required: 1 packet for 100 plants. Viability 75 per cent.

There are two ways of dealing with the crop. The seeds an be sown in a seedbed 1.5 cm (½ in) deep in rows 30 cm (1 ft) apart. Or they can be sown in peat pots or soil blocks (under cover in cold areas), putting two seeds to a pot or block, and later thinning to one. While more wasteful of seed, direct sowing can succeed in drills 1.5 cm (1½ in) deep and 60 cm (2 ft) apart. Thin the plants to 30–60 cm (1–2 ft) apart. Set out seedbed raised plants 60–75 cm (2–2½ ft) apart each way, using a garden line, trowel or dibber and plant firmly. Water in if the weather is dry. Alternatively take out a tiny trench 8–10 cm (3–4 in) deep with a draw hoe, and plant in the bottom in the damper soil. The sides of the trench protect the plants to some extent against drying out by the wind.

General cultivation Apart from hoeing, broccoli is not a demanding crop. Some plants are inclined to topple on windy sites, so earth up the stems to help avoid breakages. Top-dressing with a nitrogenous fertilizer once growth gets well under way can be most beneficial. A pinch per plant (away from the stem) is all that is required.

Weedkillers are not really necessary or desirable in small scale culture. Paraquat/diquat comes into its own on a preparatory or pre-sowing basis or for *careful* use between rows *after* planting. But in general, hoeing is adequate and much safer, though home gardeners growing on a fairly extensive scale are making more use of chemical weedkillers.

Harvesting and storing Use when ready and keep picking. By selecting suitable varieties a long season's cropping is possible. Will not store except by deep freezing, but excellent for this.

Plants per person 5   *Yield per plant* 330–450 g (12–16 oz)

Pests and diseases Common pests of all brassicas are cabbage root fly, cabbage caterpillars, cabbage aphids, cabbage white fly. Common diseases are clubroot (the most serious) and a number of other fungal diseases such as black rot, black leg, grey mould, mildew, downy mildew, damping off, bacterial leaf spot, soft spot. Also virus diseases such as mosaic, black ring spot, and deficiency troubles such as whiptail (shortage of molybdenum). See Appendix for controls.

Varieties
SPROUTING BROCCOLI Purple Sprouting Early, Purple Sprouting Late, White Sprouting Early, White Sprouting Late.
CALABRESE Pacifica (medium late), Gem (very early), Rex (early), Corvette (maincrop), Green Comet (early), Green Sprouting (late).

BRUSSELS SPROUTS
Hardy. Sprouts have become very popular in recent years. They are available over a long season which makes them almost the ideal household vegetable.

Site and soil preparation Sprouts grow best on medium to heavy firm soils, pH 6.5–7, soil index N:P:K 2–3, preferable those that have been well manured with farmyard manure or compost for the previous year, as rank soft growth is undesirable. Firm land is essential.

Exposure is of little consequence for field crops as the crop shelters itself. But on a garden scale exposure results in loosened roots and toppling and blowing over in windy weather unless some support is given, especially if the plants are of a tall, vigorous type. Where little can be done about exposure grow only the dwarfer varieties, which do best on an open site.

If the previous crop was not well manured, dig in farmyard manure or compost at 6–8 kg per m² (12–15 lb per sq yd), preferably in the autumn or very early in the year, though very rich soil is not desirable. Before sowing or planting give general fertilizer 6:9:18 at 140 g per m² (4 oz per sq yd).

Sowing and planting Seeds required: 1 packet for 100 plants. Viability 75 per cent or higher.

Early to mid-autumn sowing is still favoured in some areas, though modern hybrid sprouts are so quick-maturing that it is doubtful whether autumn sowing is really worthwhile. It is more usual to sow in cold frames in early/mid-spring (the latter for colder regions) and outdoors in seedbeds in mid-spring. Seedbed sowing is in drills 30 cm (1 ft) apart and about 1.5 cm (½in) deep, ensuring that the seedbed soil is well limed (pH 6.5) and that there is no risk of clubroot or other troubles which can sometimes necessitate resoiling or sterilizing with metham sodium in cold frames.

Plants raised in a seedbed, including those overwintered, should be planted out when large enough, in late spring or early summer, according to sowing time. Soil blocks or Jiffy 7's can also be used successfully to raise them in cold greenhouses in exposed regions. Alternatively sow seeds direct in drills outdoors from mid-spring (or earlier in mild districts) until late spring, using a precision sower or carefully placing the seeds 30 cm (1 ft) apart. Thin to 60 cm (2 ft) later. While it wastes more seeds, the time saving is considerable especially with a precision sower.

Plant out firmly with a trowel or dibber after raking or hoeing the ground to a reasonable tilth, and firming well with a roller or your feet. Plant 60–75 cm (2–2½ ft) apart each way, depending whether dwarf or tall varieties are used. Deep drills are useful in dry weather.

General cultivation Give a pinch of ammonia nitrate lime or similar (nitram or Nitro-chalk at about 6 g (¼ oz) per plant, once the plants are growing strongly. Keep away from plants' necks or they will scorch.

Birds can be a great problem in some areas, making a bird scarer or careful protection with nets or bags essential. Keep down weeds. Only water if the weather is exceptionally dry. It it better to firm the ground well around the plants or roll the ground, if possible, when the plants have wilted. Commercially, the tops of plants are pinched to encourage more even swelling of the sprouts for more intensive picking once they start forming, which has its merits in cold areas. In gardens it is doubtful if this is necessary or desirable except in the coldest areas. The lower sprouts can 'blow' in mild wet seasons or when the ground is really loose. Ridging the soil around the stem can be beneficial in exposed areas, otherwise support each plant with a cane. For weeding see Broccoli (p.45).

Harvesting and storing Once the sprouts are ready, start picking from the bottom, snapping off downwards. Frost is often said to improve their flavour. Picking can continue right through the winter, especially with late varieties. Remove all yellowing leaves regularly and take care not to loosen plants in the ground. Excellent for deep freezing.

Plants per person 5   *Yield per plant* 560 g (1 lb 4 oz)

Pests and diseases See pp.93–95 for range of insecticides and fungicides, noting that only cabbage caterpillar and rootfly are likely to be regular problems.

Varieties Peer Gynt (early dwarf; excellent crop); Topscore (early); Achilles (mid-season); Fortress (maincrop and late picking); Citadel (F1, medium late); Topscore (F1, early, medium height); Darkmar 21 (very early); Roodnerf Selection: Rido (late picking, dark green, good frost resistance); Seven Hills (late, tallish variety, medium-sized solid sprouts); Early Half Tall (Continental variety, suitable for early picking); Evesham Special, Rous Lench (solid attractive sprouts, used extensively in some market garden areas).

CABBAGE

Cabbages are excellent hardy garden vegetables, especially when grown in succession to avoid a glut. Produce a succession by choosing suitable varieties and to some extent by varying sowing times, though in practice late sowings tend to catch up with earlier ones and simply produce smaller heads.

Colewort or *Collard* is a non-hearting very hardy type of cabbage used for its leaves. *Portuguese Cabbage* is also grown for its leaves. It needs a lot of space. These, and *Red* or *Pickling Cabbage* and *Savoy*, a winter hardy type, all require similar care, as outlined below. Chinese Cabbage is more like Cos lettuce and is treated like lettuce.

Site and soil preparation Any well-drained soil except a very heavy clay. pH 6–7, soil index N:P:K 2–3. Any reasonable situation. Prepare ground by single digging. Soil should be firm. Cabbages relish a good supply of organic matter in the soil, either farmyard manure or compost, at up to 9 kg per m² (20 lb per sq yd), well dug in during the winter. If in doubt about pH always apply lime at about 280 g per m² ($\frac{1}{2}$ lb per sq yd) to be on the safe side. Before sowing or planting in growing quarters give a general fertilizer as follows: for summer, autumn, winter and savoy cabbages 8:6:12 at 140 g per m² (4 oz per sq yd); for spring cabbages 6:6:18 at 140 g per m² (4 oz per sq yd). The fertilizer can be forked or raked in over the whole area, but its high cost makes strip application attractive, when 140 g (4 oz) of fertilizer will cover a strip 2.7 m (3 yd) long by 30 cm (1 ft) wide.

Sowing and planting Seeds required: 1 very small packet of each of the different varieties. For direct seeding use 7 g ($\frac{1}{4}$ oz) per 30 m (100 ft) run for transplanting. Viability 75 per cent or higher.

Summer and Autumn cabbages are sown in an outdoor seedbed in early to mid-spring in drills 1.5 cm ($\frac{1}{2}$ in) deep and 30 cm (1 ft) apart, for planting late spring to early summer. For early crops sow in late winter in covered frames for planting out in mid-spring. *Winter cabbages* need not be sown until late spring or early summer outdoors for planting in mid-summer. Sow *Spring cabbages* in late summer for planting in mid-autumn. Plant firmly with a dibber or trowel 60 × 60 cm (2 × 2 ft) apart.

Chinese cabbage should be sown from mid-spring until mid-summer and transplanted at 60 × 60 cm (2 × 2 ft) apart when large enough. Sow *colewort* in mid-spring, then transplant or thin to 30 cm (1 ft) apart each way. Start *Portuguese cabbage* in a heated frame or greenhouse in late winter, cold frames in early spring, or outdoors in mid-spring, for transplanting 60 × 60 cm (2 × 2 ft) apart from mid-spring until early summer. Treat *red cabbage* as for Autumn/Winter cabbage. Sow *Savoy cabbage* in mid-spring for transplanting late spring/early summer. Sowing in blocks, Jiffy 7's or peat pots is a useful technique for starting superlative crops under cover without check.

It is also vital with all brassicas to use clean, disease-free soil for the seedbed, blocks or for filling peat pots to avoid spreading diseases like clubroot.

Most brassicas can be sown direct where they are to grow. Sow between mid-spring and early summer, according to variety and type.

Thin to the appropriate distance apart, keeping weeds firmly under control. Always plant brassicas firmly and use a clubroot preventive. Plants benefit from being set out in a shallow trench and earthed up later.

General cultivation Hoe regularly to control weeds. Watering may be necessary in dry spring weather to avoid checks to growth which can result in premature seeding, blackstem and other side effects.

When growth is well under way give top dressing with nitrogen scattered close to the plants at 12 g ($\frac{1}{4}$ oz) per plant (sulphate of ammonia, Nitro-chalk or similar). *Note*: overwintered Spring cabbages should not be top-dressed until they make vigorous growth in early spring. Do not top-dress late cabbage or savoys later than late summer or growth may become soft and disease-prone (botrytis). Keep the dressing clear of the stem of the plant. *Chinese cabbage* and *colewort* do not usually need top-dressing.

Clean the ground with paraquat/diquat before planting, or use this chemical *carefully* between the rows after planting.

Harvesting and storing Cut cabbages as required. Leave stumps of Spring and Summer cabbages to produce fresh green growth if you wish, otherwise clear plants as they are used.

Certain types of cabbage (especially Scandinavian) can be stored in clamps. Cabbages can be deep frozen, but this is hardly worth doing because the cropping season is so long.

Plants per person 5–10   *Yield per plant* 680 g (1 lb 8 oz)

Pests and diseases See under Broccoli.

Varieties Spring-sown pointed hearts: Hispi; Winnigstadt; Flower of Spring; Harbinger; Wheeler's Imperial; Greyhound (susceptible to splitting). Round-headed: Golden Acre, Primo (susceptible to splitting); Derby Day; Early Ballhead; Cannonball; January King. Round-headed: Delicatesse and Succession (autumn cutting); Minicole; Wiam and Standby (late autumn and early winter), January King (winter), Langendisk (cutting up to early spring); Hidena F!; Stonehead F1 (excellent keeper). Savoy: Winter King; Super Ormskirk. Autumn sown cabbage for spring cutting: Durham Early; First Early Market; First Crop; Spring Glory; Early Offenham; Avoncrest (compact); April (compact).
Red Cabbage: Langendisk Red, Volga, Red Dutch, Ruby Ball, Mammoth Red Rock (pickling).
CHINESE CABBAGE Tip Top, Canton, Wongbok.
COLEWORT Hardy Green.

CARROTS

Hardy. Another very useful vegetable indeed, which with the cultivation of early bunching (stump-rooted) crops in the protection of a cold frame, tunnel or cloche is available for the larger part of the year, especially as late crops can be stored.

Site and soil preparation Carrots undoubtedly do best in light sandy soils, but they will succeed reasonably well in most soils. pH 5.5–6, soil index N:P:K 2–3. They are not particularly affected by exposure, but love sun and moisture.

The best shaped carrots are produced in soil which has received farmyard manure or compost the previous year. Using fresh farmyard manure or compost invariable results in forked roots of coarse texture. Ground should be well dug in winter or early spring and forked and raked down to a fine, but not excessively fine, condition. A firm bed is important for good even germination. Before sowing early carrots give a general fertilizer 6:6:10–12 at 70 g per m² (2 oz per sq yd).

Sowing and planting Seed requirement: 14 g ($\frac{1}{2}$ oz) per 30 m (100 ft) row). Viability 50 per cent.

Aim to sow carrots in a firm bed in drills 30 cm (12 in) apart and 1.5 cm ($\frac{1}{2}$ in) deep when the soil is sufficiently warm. Take out drills to a line with the corner of a draw hoe and be sure to firm the soil over the drills after sowing to ensure good, even germination. Make earlier sowings in cold frames in late winter using stumpy varieties. Follow these in early spring with sowings under plastic tunnels or cloches. In early districts sowings can be made outdoors in early spring. Stump-rooted carrots can conveniently be sown broadcast, especially between a lettuce crop in a cold frame. Scatter the seeds on the soil and firm down with a spade before planting the lettuces. Forcing types of short carrots can also be sown under heated glass in mid or late winter. Due to the persistence of carrot fly, it is advisable to dust the seeds with HCH dust before sowing, or buy ready-dressed seeds.

General cultivation Intensive hoeing is helpful. Stump-rooted or short carrots need little thinning and are used for salads when very young. Thin later carrots to about 10 cm (4 in) apart, preferably when the soil is moist enough to allow this, or, as some gardeners do, simply cut off the foliage with scissors to avoid loosening the soil and letting in the carrot fly to lay its eggs. Dust with HCH or other chemical as a preventive immediately after thinning unless the seeds were dressed before sowing.

A wide range of weedkillers is available to growers. But preparing the

'Lobjoit's Green' cos is a useful self-folding variety of lettuce.

Courgettes (small marrows) are now much-valued vegetables.

land in plenty of time and applying paraquat/diquat weedkiller a day before or after sowing is the most practical way to avoid arduous weeding.

Harvesting and storing Young carrots can be pulled and used to make a tasty addition to a salad, and for freezing. Lift mature carrots in the autumn and store in sacks or (preferably) heaps of sand, where they will keep for a long time. Carrots can also be diced and bottled.

Plants per person 120   *Yield per plant* 30–60 g (1–2 oz) or more from long types

Pests and diseases Only carrot fly is likely to be really troublesome, though aphids can cause leaf distortion. Control with insecticides.

Varieties Early: Champion, Amsterdam Forcing, Scarlet Horn or Early Nantes. Maincrop: Chantenay Red-Cored or Royal Chantenay; Autumn King (resistant to carrot fly); Berjo (late); New Red Intermediate or St Valery (long exhibition varieties).

CAULIFLOWER
Half-hardy. Cauliflower is here considered separately from sprouting broccoli and is of the single-headed type. Modern breeding has now produced a wonderful range of varieties which can produce heads for a large part of the year, the exception being in wet winters, especially in colder areas. This now includes Broccoli as winter cauliflower.

Site and soil preparation Cauliflower grown best on land of fairly high fertility, well supplied with organic matter. pH 6–7, soil index N:P:K 2–3. Try to choose well-drained areas, specially for late autumn production. For earliest production seek out well-sheltered, sunny areas.

Firm land is preferable to dry, puffy soil. Do not add farmyard manure to newly ploughed or dry land. Otherwise dig in farmyard manure at 4–5 kg per m² (10–12 lb) per sq yd. Cauliflower likes rich land for quick growth, so give a balanced fertilizer 4–8:4–6:6–12 at 140 g per m² (4 oz per sq yd) before sowing or planting – lower nitrogen for early crops, high potash for later crops. Vary the rate according to the fertility of the soil.

Sowing and planting Seeds required: 1 small packet (5 g) for 100 plants. Viability 75 per cent.

The earliest crops can be sown in the protection of heated glass in mid-winter to early spring in cold frames or mid to late spring outdoors in a seedbed. For early crops sow direct into peat pots or soil blocks. The same can be done in frames, although sowing in drills 30 cm (1 ft) apart is usually more practical. Sow in drills 30 cm (1 ft) apart in outdoor seedbeds. Later varieties can be sown direct but this is wasteful of seed. Space sow in drills 60 cm (2 ft) apart.

To programme cauliflowers and obtain a succession of heads it is essential to select a range of suitable varieties (see variety list), but remember that unfavourable weather can quickly upset a timetable.

Start planting in early spring for the early crop in mild areas only after hardening off the plants carefully, and until mid-summer for the late crop. Plant them 60 cm (2 ft) apart each way, firming in and watering if the weather is dry as cauliflowers are extremely susceptible to 'buttoning' when growth is checked. Taking out a trench and planting in the base can help, provided there is sufficient depth of soil. Firm planting is essential.

General cultivation Hoeing is essential, also watering in dry conditions. Some nitrogen top dressing helps to hasten growth. Apply carefully round the neck of each plant.

Controlling weeds with weedkillers – see Cabbage.

Harvesting and storing Cut when ready (turn in some leaves to protect the developing curds). Start to cut early to avoid a glut, though cauli-flowers can be kept in eating condition for a week if hung downwards with their roots and earth left on in a cool dark shed and sprayed lightly each night. Autumn cauliflowers, if lifted just before ready can be stored for a month on the floor of a cool shed, with their roots in moist soil or sand and their leaves tied over the curds. Can be frozen whole or in sprigs, but wrap carefully to contain pervasive smell.

Plants per person 5   *Yield per plant* 0.5 kg (1 lb)

Pests and diseases See under Broccoli, but be specially careful about preventive measures against root fly at planting time.

Varieties Early Snowball, Climax (early); All the Year Round (produces large white heads and can be cut over a long period from successive sowings); Flora Blanca (original) (one of the finest autumn strains); Poulton Crown (first class curds; do not sow before late spring); White Top (autumn cutting, highly recommended); Nevada (late summer, stands up to heat and drought extremely well); Autumn Giant (improved); Majestic (Autumn Giant Selection); Novo (popular late autumn variety. Winter Cauliflower (Broccoli) – Saint Agnes (Roscoff No. 1) (should cut in mid-winter, depending on weather and situation), Saint Buryan (Roscoff No. 2) (cut in late winter).

CELERY

Half-hardy. Celery is a weed native to many coastal areas throughout the world. In its selected cultivated form it is quite fastidious, especially if the blanching types are to be grown to perfection and produce the succulent crisp undamaged leaf stalks which make celery the delicacy it is. Self-blanching celery, on the other hand, is a relatively easy crop to handle in vacant cold frames or other areas of good land.

Site and soil preparation Grows well in medium or peaty land supplied with enough organic matter to retain moisture. pH 5.5–6 or lower, soil index N:P:K 3–4. Crops can fail badly in light land which has not been given adequate attention. Soils must not lie wet, however, or growth is limited and various troubles, including slug damage, can ruin the crop. Any reasonable situation will do.

For blanching or winter celery take out a 45 cm (18 in) deep, 30 cm (12 in) wide trench for a single row of plants, or 45 cm (18 in) wide for a double row. The soil taken out is mounded up in neat banks on each side of the trench, so the trenches need to be spaced 1 m (3 ft 3 in) or so apart. Where the soil below 30 cm (1 ft) is poor it should be discarded and replaced with better top soil. Put a good deep 15–20 cm (6–8 in) layer of manure in the bottom of the trench, cover with soil and tread well to leave a firm-bottomed trench 8–13 cm (3–5 in) deep. The soil in the banks should not be levelled off and can be used for catch crops such as radish or lettuces. In good soil such elaborate preparation may not be necessary but could be limited to taking out a shallow trench and filling with manure.

For self-blanching celery dig the ground evenly and work in farmyard manure or compost during early spring digging. A vacant cold frame containing good soil can be put to good use for self-blanching celery, as it helps blanching. Some general fertilizer can be given at about 70–105 g per m² (2–3 oz per sq yd) some 10-14 days before planting, choosing a high potash value 6:9:18.

Sowing and planting Seeds required: 1 small packet gives about 100 plants. Viability 55 per cent.

Blanching celery grown outdoors requires 100–120 days from sowing to harvesting (apart from propagation). This can be speeded up considerably when it is grown under polythene tunnels or in walk-in polythene structures. As celery requires such a long growing season seeds should be sown in frames from late winter until early spring and for later crops until about mid-spring, still preferable under cover. Heated frames will be required in colder regions. Seed trays or boxes are preferable to sowing in the soil of the frame or greenhouse, which otherwise must be sterilized with heat or chemicals to avoid disease. This can obviously pose problems. Soilless composts are used in the trays or boxes or as a 7–10 cm (3–4 in) deep layer spread over the surface of the frame. Adjust the levels by removing the old soil or compost beforehand. This care is necessary because celery is extremely susceptible to various troubles in the early stages, especially damping off, which can cause a considerable loss of plants.

The compost used for seed sowing must be of good quality and well supplied with nutrients to about John Innes Seed Compost level, or a comparable soilless compost. Sow seeds very thinly and merely press them into the moist soil or compost. They can be 'chitted' before sowing by mixing with sand and keeping them moist in pans at 21°C (70°F) until they have sprouted, when they can be carefully sown. Given a temperature of 18°C (65°C), plenty of water and darkness for a few days, germination should be brisk and growth steady.

Whether seedlings are box-raised or not, they must be pricked off at about 40 per standard seed tray or 2.5–3.5 cm (1–1½ in apart) in frames. They are increasingly sown direct in peat pots, or soil or peat blocks, but germination can be difficult and it often wastes seeds, which are very tiny. Good clean soil or compost is again essential, up to John Innes No 1 standard, or a soilless equivalent. Prick off seedlings carefully, to avoid tearing or cramping their roots, and harden off plants gradually by increasing ventilation until they are ready to set out in frames for final hardening off. Frame-raised plants can also be increasingly ventilated and the lights completely removed in mid-spring.

Planting out begins in mid to late spring in plastic structures, greenhouses (for self-blanching celery) or tunnels, and in early summer outdoors in most areas. Plant carefully with a trowel. Set out plants for *blanching* celery in trenches 22–30cm (9–12 in) apart in single or double staggered rows, or 15–20 cm (6–8 in) when in single rows on the flat. *Self-blanching* celery is planted 'on the flat' in vacant frames or in plastic structures 30 cm (12 in) apart each way. It is planted closely to assist self-blanching by excluding light.

Plant only in damp soil and lift plants carefully with a good ball of soil as any check to growth at this time can be disastrous. Carefully remove all damaged leaves at planting time.

General cultivation

Blanching celery requires regular liquid feeding every 10–14 days once growth is seen to break. Use a liquid feed with a high nitrogen content. Many gardeners prefer home-made liquid manure which is simply a bag of animal manure suspended in a barrel of water.

When plants are 38 cm (15 in) high, remove any suckers or side shoots, draw the leaves together and ridge soil from the trenches around the plants. Repeat this later, and tie the tops of the plants with raffia or a rubber band. Earth up with dry soil only and be careful not to get soil inside the plant. Brown paper collars can also be used to help blanching, especially for show purposes. Keep weeds firmly under control in trenches and or on banks.

Self-blanching Celery on the flat needs a top dressing of sulphate of ammonia when the plants are 22–25 cm (9–10 in) high, and again at 35–37 cm (14–15 in). Give just a light scattering at 18 g per m² ($\frac{1}{2}$ oz per sq yd), keeping it off the plants themselves.

No earthing up is needed. Regular hoeing is essential, and the soil must never be allowed to get too dry. Clearing the land with paraquat/diquat weedkiller beforehand is helpful.

This crop will not store for salad use. Celery hearts can be frozen for cooking later, but are usually cooked, then stored in a freezer.

Pests and diseases No one trouble is generally a problem, apart from slugs, though in hot summers carrot fly can be a nuisance, causing severe wilting. Other occasional troubles are aphids, celery fly, leaf spot, root rot, pythium, late blight, soft spot, mosaic.

Varieties Lathom Self-Blanching (resistant to bolting), Avon Pearl (self-blanching), Giant White, Resistant Pink, Giant Pink.

CUCUMBER
Tender. Best results are achieved by growing entirely under glass, but cucumbers can be grown satisfactorily outdoors in mild areas, especially with the help of cloches or frames, as a follow-up crop after lettuces or other salads.

Site and soil preparation Well-drained fertile soil, pH 6, soil index N:P:K 3–4. Mild climate. Open sunny situation.

Cucumbers revel in copious organic matter and soils that retain nutrients well, so it is best to take out a trench 15–22 cm (6–9 in) deep and about 30 cm (1 ft) wide and fill it with very well-rotted manure or garden compost with a light covering of good soil to form a ridge. If the manure is on the fresh side, mix it with equal quantities of good soil. Any subsequent ridges should be made about a metre (yard) apart. Alternatively take out holes 22–30 cm (9–12in) deep and 30–36 cm (12–14in) across 60–90 cm (2–3 ft) apart and fill with pockets of manure or manure and soil. This hole method is ideal for vacant cold frames. Take out the hole under the centre of a Dutch light frame or take out two smaller holes under opposite corners of the light. Spread a base dressing of general fertilizer 12:5:6 at 140 g per m² (4 oz per sq yd) or 60 g (2 oz) per planting station evenly over the soil.

Sowing and planting Seeds required – depends on space available. Sold by number. Viability 75 per cent.

Where grown in unheated frames, under cloches or out of doors, seeds can usually be raised in an unheated greenhouse in mid-spring, though some mild heat helps to hasten germination. The best procedure for cold culture is to sow seeds singly straight in Jiffy 7s or 10 cm (4 in) peat pots filled with John Innes No. 1 potting or soilless mix. Soil blocks can also be used. Push seeds into the surface on their sides. Alternatively spread seeds between two sheets of blotting paper or wet newspaper in a shallow tray where, in a temperature of 18–21°C (65–70°F) they will germinate in 1–2 days. The viable seeds are then carefully potted up. Keep the plants in good light and harden them off for planting in frames or under cloches from late spring onwards or outdoors in early summer. Plants may need liquid feeding (see above) to keep them growing steadily. Support with a cane. Plant them with the upper surface of the pot or block above the soil and water in. Set the plants firmly in the ground, though not too firmly, 60–90 cm (2–3 ft) apart in previously prepared positions.

General cultivation Feed as necessary, about every 10–14 days. The same fertilizer used for a base feed can be scattered lightly round the plants, but *not* near their necks, provided it is watered in. In practice, it is simpler to use a liquid organic fertilizer regularly, cucumbers preferring regular rather than spasmodic supplies of food, with the emphasis on nitrogen. Top-dressing with well-rotted manure or compost is also useful once white roots are seen on the soil surface.

A coating of whitewash above plants in frames or cloches helps shield them from hot sun so they don't get scorched. Ventilate adequately on hot days. Water plants regularly with a can or hose, using a mist nozzle overhead to create a moist, muggy atmosphere.

In my own experience the only pruning necessary is keeping the plants within reasonable bounds, which depends on the space available. When plants start to grow steadily pinch out the growing point and take the leading shoots which form in the required directions. The female flowers are those at the end of the little embryo cucumbers; the males are flat with no swelling behind them and are removed. We now have all-female varieties of cucumber, grown mainly in heated greenhouses, but they can be grown without heat and yield good crops. A layer of straw on the ground is useful to prevent the cucumbers being marked. Black polythene could be used if weighted down with a few stones.

Weedkillers are not recommended, though paraquat/diquat can be used to clean up ground before setting out the plants.

Harvesting and storing Cucumbers are used when large enough. Will not store, but gherkin types excellent for pickling.

Plants per person 4–6   *Yield per plant* 2 kg (4 lb) or more, according to climate.

Pests and diseases Slugs, woodlice, collar rot, whitefly, red spider (causing yellowing of leaves) – use a range of insecticides.

Varieties Telegraph, Butcher's Disease-Resisting (for greenhouse): Conqueror (frames): Perfection (outdoor, large-fruited); Venlo (outdoor, small fruited, gherkin); Bitspot (vigorous); Femdan (All-female, greenhouse, requires little pruning and is long standing); Pepinex 69 (All-female, greenhouse, extremely prolific); Long Green Ridge (frames or outdoors).

GOURDS
Also called squashes or pumpkins, these are highly decorative with their many coloured skins. (There is also a highly ornamental but inedible

variety). The marrow is a close relation and all love organic soils and are grown in much the same way.

Site and soil preparation Soil should be of good quality, pH 5.5–6, index N:P:K 3–4. Good drainage is important. Gourds do best in a sunny spot, especially in some odd corner which is a sun trap.

Prepare the soil by local manuring, heaping well-rotted manure into holes taken out about 30 cm (1 ft) deep and about the same across. Heap a layer of good soil on top of the manure, leaving a slight mound. Space plants rather less than one metre (yard) apart each way.

Sowing and planting Seeds required – by number, according to space available. Viability 75 per cent.

Plants are best raised in 7.5 cm (3in) peat pots in a greenhouse. Push the seeds on their sides into the pot in John Innes Seed Compost or a soilless equivalent. As with all cucurbits, seeds can be germinated between a couple of sheets of blotting paper in a shallow tray and carefully potted up when just germinating. They germinate better in a temperature of 18–21°C (65–70°F), but the little plants develop very quickly and must then be kept cooler or they soon become embarrassingly large. Try to time sowings so that the plants are a reasonable size and hardened off ready to set out when all frost is past.

Cloches can be used to protect them in exposed places. When planting leave the root-ball proud of the soil and do not firm it too much. Water it in well and keep it moist until the roots get into the soil. This is specially important in hot sunny weather.

General cultivation Apart from regular watering and liberal liquid feeding the plants generally look after themselves and make rapid growth. In fact, you will need to restrict growth and to support climbers by tying them to trellis. Massive fruits can be produced for flower shows but these need to be supported with really strong netting so they are not damaged by the soil.

Chemical weedkillers are unlikely to be needed, apart from cleaning the soil before planting with paraquat/diquat or a flame gun.

Harvesting and storing Gourds must be dry before storing, and then stored in a dry, airy place. Hanging them in nets is best, and they should then last through the winter.

Plants per person 2   *Yield per plant* 2 kg (4 lb) or more

Pests and diseases Slugs, which must be dealt with firmly. Collar rot –

avoid excessive damp particularly around the neck of plant. Red spider – causes speckled leaves. Use a range of insecticides.

Varieties Large Yellow Mammoth, Hundredweight.

HERBS

Herbs are easy to grow, and fresh, dried or frozen provide a wide range of interesting and healthful flavours when preparing good food. Most thrive on reasonably good, well drained soil, in a sunny spot. The perennial kinds are reasonably hardy, but can die out in cold areas. Excessive damp is also a frequent cause of losses.

The leaves are best harvested just before the flowers open and when the plant is dry and not in full sun.

Table 3 gives the vital statistics of some of the most popular herbs. For a more detailed description of herbs, readers are referred to *How To Grow and Use Herbs* by Ann Bonar and Daphne MacCarthy (Ward Lock).

KALE OR BORECOLE

Hardy. This, the true kale, is often called poor man's fodder, as it will grow almost anywhere and in any soil. While it is not in the top rank as a succulent vegetable, it is pleasant to eat and a change from cabbage in the winter. Excellent for filling the odd corner which has not been particularly well dug or manured. If simply left to itself it produces lovely green leaves in late winter.

Site and soil preparation Kale is extremely tolerant of a wide range of soil conditions and will grow in any reasonable situation. Aim at pH 6–6.5, soil index N:P:K 1–2. Before planting give some general fertilizer at 70 g per m² (2 oz per sq yd).

Sowing and planting Seeds required: 1 small packet for 100 plants. Viability 75 per cent.

Sow the seeds in drills 30 cm (1 ft) apart from mid to late spring. Make sure the soil in the seedbed has adequate lime and is dusted with calomel to control clubroot.

Plant in late spring-early summer 60 cm (2 ft) apart in rows 60 cm (2 ft) apart. The weather can be hot and dry, so taking out a drill and planting with a dibber or trowel in the bottom of it helps to avoid drying out and encourages establishment. Using a club root preventive is also advisable – cabbage fly should be expected too.

General cultivation Very little cultivation is necessary apart from hoeing.

Text continues on p.62

Table 3. Popular Herbs – vital statistics

Herb	Life-span	Propagation	When and how	Use
Angelica	Perennial, treated as biennial	Seed	Late summer, early autumn. Transplant 45 cm (18 in) apart in rows 60 cm (2 ft) apart. Partial shade	Blanched midribs and stalks as 'celery'. Harvest mid-spring/early summer. Stalks and leaves for flavouring
Balm	Perennial	Seed or division	Mid/late spring. Transplant spring/autumn 60–90 cm (2–3 ft) apart	Fresh, frozen or dried leaves to give lemon taste or foods
Basil	Annual	Seed	Mid/late spring. Rich soil. Thin to 22 cm (9 in) by 30 cm (1 ft)	For flavouring tomato dishes in particular
Borage	Annual	Seed	Early/late spring (self seeds). Moist soil, but sun. Thin to 45 cm (18 in) by 90 cm (3 ft)	For flavouring. Freeze rather than dry
Caraway	Biennial	Seed	Mid-spring. Transplant to 15–22 cm (6–9 in) by 30 cm (1 ft). Dry soil	Gather seeds in late summer of following year for use in cakes, etc.
Chervil	Annual	Seed	Early spring/mid-autumn. Thin to 15 cm (6 in) by 30 cm (1 ft). Can be sown in boxes for winter supplies	Use young leaves for flavouring fresh or frozen. Do not allow to flower
Chives	Perennial	Seed or by division	Early spring to mid-autumn. Space 15 cm (6 in) by 30 cm (1 ft)	Flavour and garnish for salads, soup, etc. Will freeze
Dill	Annual	Seed	Early spring/early summer. Thin to 22 cm (9 in) by 45 cm (18 in)	Leaves and dried seed for flavouring. Fresh leaves can be frozen
Fennel	Perennial	Seed	Mid-spring. Transplant 30 × 30 cm (1 × 1 ft). Protect in winter	Leaves fresh or frozen for garnishing, seeds in soups, etc.

Plant	Type	Propagation	When / spacing	Uses
Garlic	Perennial	Sets (bulbs) or cloves	Early/mid-spring in 30 cm (1 ft) ... 22 cm (9 in) apart	Dry and store in late summer. Use with restraint for flavouring
Horseradish	Perennial	Sections of roots 8 cm (3 in) long	Early/mid-spring in 30 cm (1 ft) deep trench or in deep dibber holes. Spreads rapidly and becomes a weed!	To make dressings and sauces
Marjoram	Annual and perennial (two types)	Seed	Early/mid-spring. Transplant or thin to around 30 cm (1 ft) apart	Use leaves fresh, frozen or dried for flavouring
Mint (several types)	Perennial	By division	Any time, usually spring or autumn. Spacing not crucial as it spreads rapidly. Renew beds every few years or grow in boxes for winter supplies	A most useful flavouring with many uses
Parsley (see p.72)				
Rosemary	Perennial shrubby plant	Cuttings	In spring or summer. Give plenty of room	Leaves or sprigs for flavouring
Sage	Perennial	Can be grown from seed but usually cuttings	Small side shoots in frame in mid-spring. Space 60–90 cm (2–3 ft) apart	Distinctive flavouring for all protein foods – with onions and tomatoes
Savoy	Perennial	Seed	Mid-spring	Shoots for flavouring can be dried or frozen. Do not use to excess (oxalic acid)
		Division	Any time. Space out around 30 cm (1 ft)	In salads
Tansy	Perennial	Division (a weed, so watch its spread)	In spring. Space 30 × 30 cm (1 × 1 ft)	
Tarragon	Perennial	Division or cuttings in spring	Mid/late spring. Space 60 × 60 cm (2 × 2 ft) on warm, dry site	Use fresh in salads. Fresh, dried or frozen for flavouring meats
Thyme	Perennial	Seed or cuttings	Spring. Space 15 cm (6 in) by 60 cm (2 ft) in light, limed soil	Sprigs, fresh, dry or frozen for flavouring

This is a vegetable one is inclined to forget about but it is sufficiently resilient to tolerate some neglect.

For weedkillers, see Broccoli (p.45).

Harvesting and storing Cut as required throughout late winter. New growth as side-shoots develop produces a succession of leaves. Harvesting is normally brought to an end by the land being needed for new crops, especially early potatoes which can conveniently follow kale. Will not store, but young curly kale can be frozen.

Plants per person 6   *Yield per plant* 0.5 kg (1 lb)

Pests and diseases As for Broccoli.

Varieties Dwarf Green Curled, Tall Green Curled, Scotch Green Curled; Hungry Gap (sow early to late summer to crop late spring to early summer); Thousand Headed (plain leaves, very hardy); Maris Kestrel (rather large for garden culture).

LEEKS

Hardy. The leek is one of the most useful of all garden vegetables, providing supplies right through autumn, winter and early spring. This is one of the oldest vegetables known and grows as a weed in many parts of Europe. It is particularly good for cold exposed gardens where little else will thrive.

Site and soil preparation If leeks are to do well, they must have rich, deep, well-prepared, well-drained, deeply dug land. It is a waste of time to try to grow them in badly prepared, poor-textured soil. Leeks do not do well in light, sandy soil unless this is enriched with plenty of organic matter. Avoid wet, cold land. pH 5.8–6, soil index N:P:K 3–4. A sunny situation is not essential, as leeks will grow all winter in poor light.

Select a well-drained area of good soil and build it up over the years by deep digging and heavy applications of well-rotted farmyard manure or compost at 9 kg per m² (20 lb per sq yd). Dig the soil in early winter to allow the frost to break it down. Two weeks before planting in late spring to early summer fork over and firm the soil well with your feet, and work in some general fertilizer 6:6:10–12 at 140 g per m² (4 oz per sq yd). Fork this into the top 10 cm (4 in) and firm the soil again. Leaving fertilizer on the surface is a common cause of leeks failing.

Sowing and planting Seeds required: 1 small packet per 30 m (100 ft) row. Viability 75 per cent.

There are several ways of raising leeks. The simplest is to sow seeds thinly in boxes of John Innes Potting Compost No 1, or a soilless equivalent, in late winter in mild heat, and gradually harden off the plants in a cold frame in mid-spring. They germinate best when the seeds are covered with paper to stop them drying out. Pricking out seedlings into boxes is often advised but this is a waste of time. Just sow seeds very thinly to start with. Leeks can also be sown in 1.5 cm ($\frac{1}{2}$ in) deep drills 30 cm (1 ft) apart outdoors in mid-spring for a late (and smaller) crop.

The aim is to produce sturdy leek plants which can be planted out without setback. Some of the best crops result from putting out really large plants. They *can* be sown direct, without transplanting, but this wastes seeds, unless they are well spaced out.

Leeks can be planted in two ways from late spring to early summer. The first is to make 4 cm ($1\frac{1}{2}$ in) wide dibber holes about 20 cm (8 in) deep with a short steel-tipped dibber or a large crowbar at 15 cm (6 in) apart. Rows should be 30–45 cm (12–18 in) apart. Before planting trim back the roots to 1.5 cm ($\frac{1}{2}$ in) long and the tops to about 22 cm (9 in) to reduce moisture loss from the leaves and help set the plants in at full depth and make new growth quickly. Put the plants in the holes and let them drop to the bottom. Fill the holes carefully with water, but don't fill them with soil.

Alternatively take out trenches 22 cm (9 in) deep with a spade and plant the leeks in the bottom, replacing the soil gradually as for celery. Exhibition leeks are grown in barrels or through clay drainpipes to get really long blanched stems.

General cultivation Birds can be a nuisance and pull out plants. Simply replace them and protect the beds until the plants get a good grip of the ground. Leeks seldom dry out as they are deep-rooted plants, but some watering will be necessary in extreme conditions. Apply carefully to avoid filling in the holes prematurely.

They respond well to feeding with a high nitrogen liquid fertilizer. Pour this into the holes. Frequent feeding is essential for top quality leeks.

Leeks in holes will blanch themselves satisfactorily without earthing up like those planted in trenches. Paper collars are used for exhibition leeks.

Harvesting and storing Use as required, from mid-autumn until early spring or even later, depending on the need to re-use the land in spring.

Late in the season leeks can be lifted and heeled in in a shallow trench, where they will keep for a short time. They can be frozen, either blanched and sliced or cooked in white sauce.

Plants per person 24   *Yield per plant* 227 g (8 oz)

Pests and diseases Leek moth can be troublesome in some districts, causing holes in leaves – use derris (rotenone). White tip – leaves rot from the
tip. Use Bordeaux mixture. Foot rot – plants wilt and die. Change the
site for the next crop. Onion fly – grubs at base of plant cause wilting.
Use seed dressings and a range of insecticides early in season.

Varieties Hubertus, Titan (autumn-lifting); Winter Reuzen (especially
good in the North (UK)). There are many special varieties, including
local favourites such as Musselburgh.

LETTUCE
Half-hardy. Besides being one of the oldest salad vegetables in cultivation, lettuce is also the most popular, forming the centrepiece of most
salad dishes. There are four basic types: 1) cabbage or hearting, 2) bunching – hearting cabbage types with curly leaves, 3) cos type with lance-
shaped leaves, 4) cutting types forming rosettes of leaves (American
type). Breeding has mixed these basic types so the trade now offer 1)
plain-leaved butterhead (hearting) types, 2) crisp-headed varieties (curly
leaves), 3) winter cabbage lettuce, 4) summer cos (lance-shaped leaves), 5)
winter cos (semi-cos), 6) forcing cabbage varieties, 7) cutting or leaf
types.★
★Not so readily available in U.K.
    Many gardening books state that lettuces can be cropped the whole
year round, from late spring to mid-autumn outdoors and late autumn to
mid-spring protected by glass or polythene structures. This may be true
in mild areas with good light, but it can be difficult to produce worthwhile lettuces during the winter in colder areas where light is poor too
and humidity is high, causing rapid deterioration. But modern breeding
has done much to improve lettuce varieties which will grow well in the
heat of summer and the cold, damp and poor light of winter.
    Lettuces normally grown out of doors are dealt with here.

Site and soil preparation Lettuces seem able to stand up reasonably well to
growing in the same place year after year. They also tolerate a wide range
of soils, though the best are grown on medium to light, rich, well-dug
land, for lettuces, though not a greedy crop, do not have large roots and
cannot forage for food like other crops. They will grow in heavier land
too, provided this is well drained. Lettuces love sun but are reasonably
tolerant of cool temperatures and, being a low-growing crop, are
remarkably tolerant of exposure. However, the earliest crops are always
picked from the sunniest, most sheltered beds.
    Lime is essential for good lettuces and the pH must be between 6.5 and

7. Do not go above pH 7 or nutritional problems could arise. Soil index N:P:K 2-3-4. Incorporate farmyard manure or well-made compost when digging or rotovating. Fertilizers for spring and summer crops should be balanced 12.8.12 and used at 70 g per m² (2 oz per sq yd).

Sowing and planting Seeds required: 30 g (1 oz) for a 30 m (100 ft) row. Viability 80 per cent.

Pelleted or pilled seeds are available. Split pills open on germination to avoid the risk of rotting which sometimes occurs in the larger types of pellets.

The earliest outdoor crops are produced from pelleted or split pill seeds sown thinly in boxes or individually in small paper or peat pots in heated greenhouses. Pellets germinate best on the surface, but bare seeds are best lightly covered. Keep boxes or pots covered until seeds germinate, which they do best at about 18°C (65°F), though satisfactorily at lower temperatures. Lettuces *do not* germinate well in high temepratures. Use John Innes Seed Compost or a soilless equivalent for sowing. After germination, give plants all the light available.

Sowing time varies from mid-winter to early spring according to region, so you can plant out as soon as the ground is reasonably warm (from early spring in warm regions to mid-spring in colder ones). After germination it takes 4–6 weeks to produce fair-sized lettuces for planting outdoors. How long one can hold back the lettuces before planting out depends on temperature. It is best to get the lettuces into cold frames as soon as possible, or at least stand them out in a sheltered spot for 2–3 weeks before planting out.

Greenhouse-raised lettuces can be planted 2–3 weeks earlier under frames or cloches to mature earlier. Space them 20 × 20 cm (8 × 8 in) apart in frames or cloches (two rows per standard cloche, though three rows are possible). Outdoors they should be 20–22 cm (8–9 in) apart in rows 30 cm (1 ft) apart. Here is a summary of the process:

Sow in greenhouse	Into frame	Plant out	Ready for use
Mid-winter at 16–18°C (60–65°F) (germinate in 10–14 days)	for 3–4 weeks	Early/mid-spring (2–3 weeks earlier under cloches)	Late spring
Late winter, cold	for 3–4 weeks	Mid-spring	Late spring/early summer

Sow outdoors from early spring to mid-summer at 2–3 week intervals for cutting the same year, and in mid-autumn for overwintering outdoors or in frames to mature in spring at a time which will depend much on the region in which they are grown, though usually late spring.

A firm seed bed is essential. Use bare seeds, pelleted or pilled seeds and space-sow with a precision seeder or, more tediously, by hand. Make drills 1.5 cm ($\frac{1}{2}$ in) deep and at least 30 cm (1 ft) apart. Sow pellets 6–15 cm ($2\frac{1}{2}$–6 in) apart, then thin as required. The whole object of using pelleted seed is to avoid thinning, but germination can be poor if the seedbed is not firm or moist enough or if the weather is too wet. So many gardeners prefer the sometimes surer germination of bare seeds and are prepared to thin. It can cost less too! Aim to have the lettuces growing 22–30 cm (9–12 in) apart, according to type, variety and eventual size. Plant them out firmly to a line, using a trowel.

General cultivation Deal with weeds. Watering may be required, especially for early planted lettuces if the spring is very dry. Some feeding with nitrogen such as Nitro-chalk or sulphate of ammonia will usually be needed. Keep it off the leaves. It is best applied during rainy weather or before watering.

Lettuces take longer to develop as the season progresses and may struggle to germinate in high summer, certainly for the latest sowings. The autumn-sown crop outdoors must be carefully looked after. Control slugs, which can do a lot of damage by eating the lettuces and letting in diseases.

Cos lettuces still sometimes need blanching to produce good quality heads – tie the leaves together 10–14 days before harvesting – but modern varieties are claimed to be self-blanching. Cos lettuces of the winter type do not need blanching.

American type non-hearting lettuces from which leaves are continuously pulled for salads are treated in much the same way as hearting lettuces.

Harvesting and storing Cut lettuces when required. It pays to start really early with young lettuces, otherwise one ends up with a glut and spoilt plants will not store.

Plants per person 10–20　　　　　　　*Yield per plant* up to 340 g (12 oz)

Pests and diseases Slugs are the main problem of this short-term crop – use slug pellets regularly. Root aphids – clusters of white mealy aphids are seen at roots, causing wilting. Water with malathion. For other troubles, change site and select varieties carefully.

Varieties Plain-leaved butterhead types – Newmarket (hearts attractive golden green; quick maturing); Poulton Market (earlier, slightly larger edition of Newmarket); Avondefiance (leaves semi-crisp, resistant to tip burn, botrytis and downy mildew in autumn); Borough Wonder; Buttercrunch; Cobham Green; Kares (summer, resistant to tip burn and five Dutch races of mildew). May King (quick-growing early crop); Reskia (summer); Suzan (larger, earlier type of Trocadero); Tom Thumb (small compact heads); Trocadero Improved. *Crisp headed* – Avoncrisp (resistant to downy mildew and root aphids; Great Lakes (slow maturing, solid heart, slow to bolt); Minetto (small); New York (large); Penlake (crinkly leaves); Webb's Wonderful (large curled). *Winter Cabbage types* – Imperial Winter (large); Valdor (resistant to cold weather); Winter Marvel (bright green solid heart). *Summer cos varieties* – Little Gem (crisp, compact, semi-cos); Lobjoit's Green Cos (self-folding, dark green); Paris White (self-folding). *Winter cos* – Winter Density (dark green, semi-cos). *Forcing or frame cabbage types* – Dandie (for frost-free or heated houses, cutting through winter, fast growing); Magnet (suitable for unheated glass, large-leaved, solid-hearted); Mayfair (for cold frames); Ravel (Type 50) (quick-growing, cropping all winter, easy to grow in cooler conditions).

MARROW and COURGETTES

Tender/half-hardy. While not everyone's favourites as vegetables they are interesting plants to grow for show purposes. Their culture is generally similar to gourds and there are two basic types, trailing and bush. Courgettes, now a very popular vegetable, are just small marrows.

Site and soil preparation Any reasonable soil, but must be well drained and made deep and rich. pH 5.5–6, soil index N:P:K 2–3. Marrows will stand a little shade, so the odd corner can be used, provided the soil is suitable.

Improving the soil locally with manure or compost helps by saving time and effort. Dig the soil to a reasonable depth and improve it with a good forkful of manure at each planting station. Cover with a layer of soil, leaving small depressions. Space plants about one metre (1 yd) apart each way. Use general fertilizer 12:12:16 locally at 70 g per m² (2 oz per sq yd), which works out at about 30 g (1 oz) per mound.

Sowing and planting Seeds required: bought by number. Viability 75 per cent.

Seeds are best raised in mild heat in 7.5–10 cm (3–4 in) peat pots of John Innes Potting Compost No 1 or a soilless equivalent. Push two seeds into each pot in mid-spring. Sow in cold frames slightly later, or out of doors in late spring. An inverted jam jar is useful to help germination out of doors. Like all cucurbits, the seeds can be germinated between two sheets of damp blotting paper, potting up the seeds as soon as they are seen to be breaking – possibly 48–50 hours at 18°C (65°F). Harden off the plants in late spring or early summer, aiming to get sturdy but not over-large plants. Plant them in the prepared positions with the root-ball proud of the soil. Water plants well before planting, and water in and keep them watered for a day or two, but not saturated or their stems could rot. A cloche is useful to protect them for a few days. While marrows can be grown in cold or heated glasshouses or plastic structures, they grow so well outdoors that it is a waste of good under-cover space. If they *are* to be grown under cover, advance the planting programme by 3–6 weeks and grow them similarly in heaps of manure as they are gross feeders.

General cultivation Watering is the main chore, especially until plants develop a good root system. Keep trailing kinds trained or supported a little or they become wild. Assist pollination by dusting pollen from flat-bodied male flowers on to the female flowers with their embryo marrows behind. Alternatively, remove male flowers completely and insert in female flowers. If large marrows are wanted leave only 3–4 per plant to mature fully. If you are growing for courgettes take these as they develop, to encourage further growth.

Regular feeding with a high nitrogen fertilizer is advised, especially when the fruits are beginning to swell.

Harvesting and storing Cut when required. Best size is 22–30 cm (9–12 in) long for a good flavoured marrow and about 12–15 cm (5–6 in) for a tender courgette. The larger, fully matured marrows can be stored for use during the winter in a cool, dry, frost-free shed, preferably hung up in nets so there is a good flow of air around them. Small marrows or courgettes can be deep frozen.

Plants per person 2   *Yield per plant* 2 kg (4 lb)

Pests and diseases As for cucumber

Varieties A wide range of *bush, trailing* and *courgette* types is available, many of them Fl hybrids, e.g. Green Bush (courgette), Early Gem, Long Green (trailing, straight, extra large), Emerald Cross (similar to Early Gem but with mottled fruit with faint stripe), Zucchini (early, stripe free, also excellent courgette), All Green Bush (can be cut early as a courgette cr allowed to mature), Custard White (bush), Long White (trailing), White Bush (smaller).

MUSHROOMS (Psalliota campestris)

Mushrooms can be grown in the open air but they are much more often grown under cover in sheds, cellars or basements. They are a specialist crop – see *Complete Book of the Greenhouse*, I.G.Walls.

ONIONS

Hardy. A very old vegetable indeed, and certainly very valuable, as it provides food throughout the winter. Not every gardener succeeds with onions, mainly because they like good rich deep soil, plenty of sun and a long growing season.

Site and soil preparation Medium to light soils, pH 5–5.6, soil index N:P:K 2–3–4. Avoid very heavy or very light soils. Good drainage is absolutely essential if fungal troubles are to be avoided. Sun is essential for ripening. It is a common mistake to choose a bed which loses sun quickly during the autumn.

Permanent beds, built up over the years by deep cultivation and adequate supplies of organic matter, are highly desirable though not essential for good results. Pests and diseases specific to onions can build up, eventually making it necessary to move the bed, but onions could only be rotated around the garden like other crops where the soil is particularly good.

Onions like rich deeply dug land, so make every effort to provide this. Incorporate plenty of *old* organic matter, up to 15 kg per m² (30 lb per sq yd). It is not generally appreciated how deeply onion roots penetrate, since they are thought of as a surface crop because their bulbs form there. After digging put on fertilizer 6:6:18 at 140 per m² (4 oz per sq yd). While the need for phosphorus and potash is emphasized in the fertilizer programme, lack of nitrogen can cause considerable trouble in the crop. After giving fertilizer firm the bed with your feet then rake it down to a fine tilth for sowing or planting. Just before sowing or planting give a dusting of dried soot if available (but *not* from an oil-fired chimney).

Sowing and planting Seeds required: 28 g (1 oz) per 30 m (100 ft) row. Viability 70 per cent.
There are three methods of growing onions.
Method 1 From seeds sown in mid-winter in gentle heat under glass in John Innes Seed Compost or a soilless equivalent. Prick off into boxes, 40 or so per standard seed tray, in John Innes Potting Compost No 1 or a soilless equivalent. The plants are then grown cool and hardened off for planting outdoors during mid to late spring according to region. Plant with a line and trowel with the little bulbs *just at soil level* (not below or

well above). The plants must be firm and spaced 15 cm (6 in) apart in rows 30 cm (12 in) apart.

Method 2   Sow thinly direct in the open in drills 1.5 cm ($\frac{1}{2}$ in) deep with the soil well firmed over the seeds, between late winter and mid-spring. Seeds can also be sown outdoors in late summer or early autumn in milder regions, though they are difficult to overwinter in wet areas. Germination is invariably poor if soil is not firmed well after sowing. Thin gradually to 5–15 cm (2–6 in) apart, depending whether small or large onions are required. Commercially onions are grown close together to give small ripe bulbs, but many gardeners aim to grow large bulbs for flower shows. Thinnings can be used as spring or salad onions.

Method 3   From onion sets. These are small onions produced from broadcast sowings in late spring of the previous year on poorish land, often under cloches, to give small, very ripe bulbs. In early to mid-spring the sets are planted, half covered, in well-prepared ground spaced 15 cm (6 in) apart in drills 30 cm (1 ft) apart. Birds often pull out the sets, especially once the leaves start to form, so provide some protection until they get a firm hold on the ground.

General cultivation   Hoe regularly. Do not start watering unless the weather is really dry. Onions can stand fairly dry conditions, which is why they do so well in the Mediterranean region. The fertilizers and manures given when preparing the soil should sustain smaller onions throughout the season. For larger bulbs use a liquid feed high in nitrogen every 14 days. But quality and taste tend to be impaired when bulbs are blown up in this way.

Paraquat/diquat weedkiller is likely to be useful for cleaning land before planting.

Harvesting and storing   When the bulbs begin to turn brown, usually in early autumn, ease them slightly out of the ground with a fork. The tips can also be tied over or, as some gardeners do, simply give the stem a good nip above the bulb with the fingers. Finally, lift the bulbs on a good day and spread them out on wire netting (above a cold frame is a convenient place) to get as much sun as possible. Their keeping qualities depend on the ripeness of the bulb, hence the high quality of Spanish bulbs.

Store only the best onions, removing any soft, damaged or open-necked ones to use as soon as possible. Pack in single layers in shallow boxes or hang up in nets in a cool, airy, frost-free hut or cellar. Traditionally they are made into 'ropes', an operation better learnt by demonstration than by description. Can also be frozen chopped or sliced.

Plants per person 15   *Yield per plant* 56–114 g (2–4 oz)

Onion 'Ailsa Craig', an old and reliable variety, is still among the best for winter storage.

Parsley, useful alike for flavouring and decorating food, can be grown as well in a pot as in the open ground.

Pests and diseases Onions are not normally subject to serious problems, but there is a longish list of possible troubles. Onion fly – grubs eat into the base of the plant (the most likely problem). Use seed dressings on seed-raised plants. Botrytis and mildews – regular use of fungicides advisable. When failure cannot be accounted for, grow them on a new site in future.

Varieties Lancastrian (exhibition, when available); Hygrow F.1 Hybrid (high quality, keeps well); Balstora (heavy-yielding early crop); Jumbo (large straw-coloured bulbs); Rijnsburger (excellent keeper); Robusta (golden coloured, thin-skinned); Ailsa Craig (large); Bedfordshire Champion (large globe-shaped bulbs); Paris Silver Skin (small bulbs lifted early are right size for bottling); Winter Over or Winter Hardy White Lisbon (only suitable for autumn sowing); White Portugal (medium-sized flat white bulb used for pickling or bunching for salad work); Stuttgart Giant (best general-purpose onion sets).

Pickling Onions Hardy. The small, white, silver-skinned bulbs for pickling are not sown until mid-spring. Sow thinly in 1.5 cm ($\frac{1}{2}$ in) deep drills. Lavish preparation of the soil is not necessary, merely normal digging and the fertilizer recommended for onions. Lift them when young and tender and prepare for pickling.
Varieties Stuttgart Giant; Barletta, Queen (cocktail); Pompeii (earliest and smallest cocktail).

Potato Onions Treat like shallots, which see.

Salad or Spring Onions Hardy. These are grown in a similar way to ordinary bulb onions, but intensive soil preparation is not necessary provided fertilizer is given as for ordinary onions. Sow in succession from late winter to late spring and again in late summer to overwinter in drills 1.5 cm ($\frac{1}{2}$ in) deep and 30 cm (1 ft) apart. Sow thickly, 230 g (8 oz) per 30 m (100 ft) row. The soil *must* be firmed over the seeds or germination can be very patchy. Pull the onions as required to produce a succulent salad ingredient. Salad onions can be grown to perfection in plastic structures, sown in late winter to early spring.
Variety White Lisbon.

PARSLEY
Half-hardy. Though classed as a herb, parsley merits full instructions like the vegetables.

Site and soil preparation Any good, well-drained soil, but it must be deep. pH 6–6.5, soil index N:P:K 2–3. Any reasonable situation, not cold or low-lying. Some shade will do no harm, especially in summer.

As a close relative of the carrot, parsley likes similar growing conditions (but can stand some shade). Good deep soil, well dug and reasonably fertile but with no fresh animal manure, are the main requirements. Good drainage is absolutely essential, as parsley is certain to fail in wet, soggy land. Dig ground one spit deep and break down to a good tilth with a fork. Before sowing apply a 10:7:10 general fertilizer at 70 g (2 oz) per sq yd. Some soot or wood ash, if available, is desirable to darken it and improve its food value.

Sowing and planting Seeds required: 7 g ($\frac{1}{4}$ oz) per 30 m (100 ft) row. Viability 60–70 per cent.

Sow seeds in early to mid-spring and again in mid-summer in drills 1.5 cm ($\frac{1}{2}$ in) deep and about 30 cm (1 ft) apart. Thin to about 20 cm (8 in) after the rather slow germination typical of this crop. Seeds can also be sown in boxes under cover in late winter to early spring and pricked out at 50 per seed tray, for planting in mid to late spring 20 cm (8 in) apart in rows 30 cm (1 ft) apart. Can also be grown in pots. Parsley seeds are notorious for poor germination unless sown in well-compacted ground and uniformly firmed. Dress the seeds with HCH before sowing to help prevent carrot fly attack.

General cultivation Regular hoeing is required, coupled with watering, particularly in a hot summer as parsley can suffer severely from drying out, especially if not in shade. Firming the soil helps to conserve moisture. A little pinch of sulphate of iron and magnesium sulphate (Epsom salts) can give the parsley a really rich colour. Cloche protection in the autumn will extend the picking season considerably.

Control weeds as for carrots but weedkillers are unlikely to be required in home gardens.

Harvesting and storing Pick as required, a little from each plant, especially in early autumn to encourage a further flush of growth for the winter. Parsley sprigs can be frozen or dried.

Plants per person 3–4   *Yield per plant* 140–170 g (5–6 oz)

Pests and diseases Carrot fly, violet root rot, leaf spot. See Appendix.

Varieties Moss Curled and Paramount, Bravour.

PARSNIP

Hardy. This is a very old vegetable. It is not everybody's favourite but those who like it consider it a delicacy.

Site and soil preparation The very nature of this long-rooted vegetable demands a really deep, stone-free soil, well-drained and of good texture. pH 6, soil index N:P:K 2–3. Will grow in any reasonable situation.

Ground should be deeply dug, or holes taken out every 37 cm (15 in) with a crowbar to a depth of 45–60 cm (18–24 in) and filled with equal parts of soil and sand. Use no fresh manure, land which has been manured previously being ideal. Before sowing apply fertilizer 12:12:20 at 70 g per m² (2 oz per sq yd) and fork in well. Where bore holes are used, mix some fertilizer into the mixture *before* filling the holes with it.

Sowing and planting Seeds required: 14 g (½ oz) per 30 m (100 ft) row. Viability 70 per cent.

Parsnip seeds must be sown early to give a long season of growth. Late winter to early spring is the usual time, depending on soil conditions. Sow the large flat seeds in groups of three or four, at 20 cm (8 in) intervals in drills 37 cm (15 in) apart or in the bore holes. Later thin to one seedling per station. Sowing a row of radishes or lettuces *in* the rows of this slow-germinating vegetable marks them making it possible to hoe early without damaging the young parsnips.

General cultivation Regular hoeing is all that is generally required. Parsnips are such a deep-rooted crop that they seldom suffer from shortage of moisture.

Hoeing and hand weeding are usually sufficient to control weeds in home gardens.

Harvesting and storing Lifting does not usually begin before late autumn after frost, which sweetens the roots and greatly improves their quality. The roots can be left in the ground until required, protecting them only in very severe weather with straw. Roots still in the ground when the next season begins can be lifted and stored for a while in sand in a cool shed or cellar.

Plants per person 6–8   *Yield per plant* Very variable – up to 1 kg (2 lb)

Pests and diseases Carrot fly, canker, mildew, vein diseases. To avoid canker use resistant varieties. See also under Carrot.

Varieties Avonresister (medium-sized roots, fairly resistant to canker); Hollow Crown (long tapering roots); Lisbonnais (exhibition stock, long clean attractive roots); Offenham (broad-shouldered, suitable for shallow soils); Tender and True (good large heavy roots).

PEAS

Hardy/half-hardy. One of the most useful vegetables for eating fresh or storing in a deep freeze. Also a very old vegetable which probably accounts for the hundreds of varieties available. There are two main types, round-seeded and wrinkled, the former being earlier and hardier than the latter. There are more dwarf varieties of the wrinkled than the round, while the round tend to be the heavier croppers.

Site and soil preparation Peas are reasonably tolerant of different soils apart from very heavy soils which can be cold and damp, rotting the seeds before they germinate. Foot and neck rot also seem more troublesome on heavy land. Peas like good drainage and deeply dug soil, pH 6.5–7, soil index N:P:K 1–3. Light soils can dry out badly, which does not suit peas, so the trench system is then used, with layers of organic matter built up beneath the peas. They like a sunny, not too exposed situation.

Unless the trench system is followed, dig deeply, incorporating well-rotted farmyard manure or compost at a rate of 10 kg per m² (20 lb per sq yd). Before sowing fork in a 6:10:17 general fertilizer at 50 g per m² (1½ oz per sq yd). Otherwise dig trenches about 30 cm (1 ft) deep in autumn and fill to within 15 cm (6 in) of the surface with well-rotted organic matter. If trenches are opened in the autumn they can be used for garden rubbish. Fill in the trench with soil over the organic matter and fork over the surface before firming and raking ready for sowing. *Do not use grass cuttings that have been treated with weedkiller.* Use fertilizer at the same rate as above, though some gardeners favour lower applications in trenches. Avoid contact between peas and fertilizer by rubbing in the fertilizer with your foot before sowing.

Sowing and planting Seeds required: 450 g (1 lb) per 30 m (100 ft) row. Viability 80 per cent.

For extra-early crops in mild areas in lighter soils sow from mid-winter to early spring. Usually, especially in northern areas, early to mid-spring is soon enough. Sowings can also be made from late spring to mid-summer.

Sow seeds 5–7.5 cm (2–3 in) deep in flat-bottomed drills 15 cm (6 in) across, taken out with a draw hoe. Space out peas on the base of the drill

5–7.5 cm (2–3 in) apart, in fives. Space rows according to height: 60 cm (2 ft) apart for dwarf varieties, about twice that for tall varieties. Peas can also be sown in single V-shaped drills 15 cm (6 in) apart, but the flat-bottomed drill method is better. Really early crops can be sown in 5 cm (2 in) peat pots in early to mid-winter for planting out when the weather is suitable, usually in early spring. Be sure to grow the peas very cool or they will become tall and lanky. Sowings can also be made under cloches in early to mid-winter in *mild* areas, but cloches are usually used to forward crops by some 2 – 3 weeks. Use thiram seed dressings for early sowings and take precautions against birds, which love the succulent leaves, by using nets or black thread.

General cultivation Weeding carefully with the fingers between the plants may be the first job, followed by putting in some form of support. Dwarf peas *can* be grown without any support, but this is seldom very satisfactory. Good beech twigs give ideal support. Push them in some 10 cm (4 in) from the outside of the rows, then cut off the tops and put these in the ground at the bottom of the twigs to start the peas climbing. See that the sticks are tall enough for the variety grown. A row of stakes and wire netting can be useful, and for really tall peas there is no substitute for tall stakes and nylon nets. Peas demand quite a lot of time and care, especially for supporting them.

Peas *may* need watering but this is where the trench system has a lot in its favour, as the organic matter under the peas holds moisture beautifully, even in a dry summer. Do not let the peas blow about, especially after wind and rain, or their stems will get irreparably crimped.

Chemical weedkilling is seldom practical in gardens. Much better to start with clean ground.

Harvesting and storing Pull when required, starting early with the succulent young pods rather than waiting until there is a glut of full ones. Peas are ideal for deep freezing.

Plants per person 15 – 20   *Yield per plant* Variable, up to
                                              250 g (8.75 oz)

Pests and diseases While there is an imposing list of possible troubles, peas are generally fairly trouble free if the site is changed regularly and seed dressings are used to prevent damping off. Use a range of insecticides for other sucking and biting pests as required.

Varieties Round seeded: Feltham First (very early dwarf, hardy); Meteor (hardy first-early, for autumn or spring sowings); Pilot (medium large pointed pods); Superb (second early, large slightly curved pods). First early wrinkled: Kelvedon Wonder (dwarf, heavy cropper, fine flavoured); Little Marvel (excellent heavy cropper); Progress No. 9 (large podded). Maincrop: Early Onward (blunt, dark green pods, produces freely); Hurst Greenshaft (early maincrop, high yielding, sweet flavoured, suitable for freezing); Lincoln (prolific, pointed pods, sweet flavoured); Onward (prolific mid-season dwarf, large blunt pods).

PEAS, Asparagus

Half-hardy. These are a bushy type of pea unrelated to the familiar garden pea, with rectangular pods which are cooked whole. Culture is basically similar to that for garden peas, but sow in early to mid-spring in drills 1.5 cm ($\frac{1}{2}$ in) deep and 60 cm (2 ft) apart. Thin to 30 cm (1 ft) apart in the drills. Pick the pods when young and tender. Asparagus peas grow 45 cm ($1\frac{1}{2}$ ft) high but sprawl a good deal and require firm support with posts and string.

POTATOES

Half-hardy. No other vegetable is more extensively used round the world. It is one of the top five world food crops and the most common source of carbohydrate in the diet. It can be stored for long periods.

Site and soil preparation Potatoes will grow in most soils provided a suitable variety is chosen for that soil. Ideally the soil should be medium to light, free draining and well exposed to the sun, pH 5.5–6, soil index N:P:K 2–3. Potatoes do not need excessively deep cultivation and can grow well even in shallow soils, though best results follow thorough digging or ploughing 30 cm deep (1 ft). They make an excellent 'cleaning crop' for dirty land because of all the cultivation involved and the blanketing effect of the foliage. Any reasonable situation will do, but avoid frost pockets.

While potatoes respond to fairly heavy applications of manure or compost at up to 10 kg per m² (20 lbs per sq yd), this does tend to encourage slug damage on heavier soils, so one cannot say categorically that organic matter should be given in the year of cropping. Where slugs are a problem, it is better to grow on land manured for a previous crop. This also applies to trench growing. For early potatoes apply fertilizer 10:10:12 at 140 g per m² (4 oz per sq yd). For second earlies and late potatoes apply 6:10:12 fertilizer at the same rate. Fertilizer can be broadcast before planting but in gardens it is more effective to scatter it along the bottom of the open drill, then cover it with soil so it is not in direct contact with the seed potatoes. *Do not give lime* unless the ground is very acid indeed, as this will encourage scab disease.

Sown early, parsnips should yield a heavy crop of roots, sweet-tasting once they have experienced a few frosts.

Sowing and planting Seeds required: 6 kg (14 lb) per 30 m (100 ft) drill. Viability 95–100 per cent.

Potatoes are grown from seed tubers which should be certified as reaching a high standard of trueness to type and freedom from disease. Some gardeners prefer to save their own seed potatoes, selecting sound medium-sized tubers from the previous crop, but this cannot be done for many years because the stock deteriorates. Small seed potatoes are best, though large ones can be cut lengthwise, so that each section bears sprouts. Dust the exposed cuts with flowers of sulphur, *not* lime.

Early potatoes are best sprouted in a light frost-free place under artificial light if necessary. Indeed all potatoes can be sprouted, though it is not really essential for mid-season or late types. Adequate sprouting takes some weeks.

There are several ways of planting potatoes. 1) Take out trenches

10–12 cm (4–5 in) deep with a spade or draw hoe when the soil is friable enough. Put down a line for guidance. 2) Plant 10–12 cm (4–5 in) deep with a trowel or dibber in flat ground or ground which has been previously ridged.

Earlies and second-earlies should be planted in late winter to early spring about 30 cm (1 ft) apart in rows 50–60 cm (20–24 in) apart. Mid-season and maincrop go in from early to late spring at about 37 cm (15 in) spacing in rows 60 cm (2 ft) apart or more. With modern vigorous varieties there is no need to reduce the sprouts to three or four. Plant with sprouts upwards.

Extra earlies can be grown under heated or cold glass. Put them in the ground inside the greenhouse, or in pots or boxes of soil, allowing sufficient space, e.g. two potatoes to a 25 cm (10 in) pot. Watering is essential for those grown under cover.

Some of the early potatoes planted normally can be covered with polythene or glass cloches to speed their development. But remember that these cloches will not necessarily protect their tender shoots from frost unless straw or other insulating material is used.

To grow potatoes by Method 3, under a black polythene mulch, take out shallow depressions 5–8 cm (2–3 in) deep and 60 cm (2 ft) apart and lay the polythene over them, anchoring it with earth at the edges. (Buy polythene wide enough to cover about three drills). Make small slits in the polythene and push in the tubers 30–35 cm (12–14 in) apart, preferably sprouting them well beforehand. The leaves will soon find their way to the light through the slits, though a few of the shoots which develop under the polythene may need to be pulled through. The potatoes form in the dark under the polythene, a trouble-free method of growing them.

General cultivation Hoeing is often recommended, but there is no need to hoe to control weeds if paraquat/diquat was used to clean the ground in the first place. Fastidious gardeners earth up several times through the season, to protect young tender foliage when there is a risk of frost damage. Alternatively shoots can be protected under straw or polythene. Watering will only be necessary in a very dry season.

In many years of growing potatoes on a garden scale I have found paraquat/diquat an excellent weedkiller for this crop, used as the shoots break through the ground. It can also be used between the rows. Paraquat/diquat avoids bringing soil down from the ridge as happens when you hoe.

Harvesting and storing Potatoes are ready when their foliage turns yellow and the tubers are large enough to use: earlies in early to mid-summer (according to district), mid-season following in late summer and lates in early or mid-autumn. Potatoes often have to be got out of the ground as soon as possible to avoid slug damage. The foliage (haulm) can be cut off before lifting if necessary. When lifting potatoes use a broad-pronged fork so that as little damage is done as possible. Try to lift on a dry day so that the skin of the potatoes is dry. Do not leave them lying around in a light place or they will turn green.

Modest quantities of potatoes can be stored in sacks, bins or boxes. Avoid polythene bags, which cause sweating. Potatoes store best in cool frost-proof stores, garages or cellars. Pits 22–30 cm (9–12 in) deep can be dug out of the ground in a dry spot and lined with a deep layer of straw. Heap the potatoes into a pile 60–75 cm (2–3 ft) high and cover with straw, then with a fair layer of soil. The pit can be opened as required. Check that mice are not active. Do not store any obviously decayed or diseased potatoes as these quickly spread trouble, and look over potatoes in store regularly.

Plants per person 25 – 30   *Yield per plant* 2.5–3.5 kg (6–8 lb)

Pests and diseases Scab disease, blight and neck rot. Most troublesome pests are eelworm and slugs, the former demanding rotation, the latter slug pellets.

Note: EEC Regulations do not permit the *sale* of certain varieties of potato.

Varieties (all immune to wart disease)
Earlies Home Guard (white, heavy cropper, good cooking, salad, exhibition). Ulster Sceptre (white, good cropping, cooking, salad); Pentland Javelin (white, heavy cropping, eelworm and virus resistant, good cooking, exhibition).
Second earlies Maris Peer (white, currently best cropper, good cooking, salad, resistance to blight); Red Craigs Royal (good all-rounder); Ulster Classic (minimal waste, good dry cooking, exhibition).
Maincrop Maris Piper (white all-rounder, eelworm resistance, scab and slugs can cause problems); Record (yellow, quality cooker, stores well); Desiree (yellow, bright red skin, outstanding yield, first-class baking, roasting, frying, susceptible to scab and slugs); Golden Wonder (late maturing, floury dry cooking, unsurpassed keeping quality, but lower yields).
Salad types (besides those mentioned) Pink Fir Apple; Aura (yellow); Purple Congo, Red Cardinal (coloured throughout).

RADISH

Hardy. This very useful salad crop must be harvested young, so it lends itself to successional sowings. It can be grown outdoors or under glass or polythene protection and is often grown as a catch crop between rows of lettuces or other crops.

Site and soil preparation Radishes like the lighter types of soil, well-drained, warm and fertile, pH 6.5–7, soil index N:P:K 2–3. Choose a sunny situation with some protection from cold winds. Avoid weedy ground.

Prepare the soil in the normal way, avoiding fresh applications of farmyard manure. Peat is ideal for forking into the top 5 cm (2 in) of soil to improve its texture. Make the seedbed firm with your feet. Radishes are often said to need no fertilizers but unless the soil is already very fertile give a 10:7:10 fertilizer at 50 g per m² ($1\frac{1}{2}$ oz per sq yd) before each sowing, raking it into the soil surface.

Sowing and planting Seeds required: 28 g (1 oz) per 30 m (100 ft) row, sown broadcast at 28 g per 2.5 m² (1 oz per 3 sq yd). Viability 75 per cent.

Sow the seeds thinly in drills 1.5 cm ($\frac{1}{2}$ in) deep and 22–30 cm (9–12 in) apart, or more conveniently broadcast them on the surface, firming them on the soil with the flat of a spade. When sowing between existing lettuces or other crops, simply scatter the seeds and let them lie on the surface. They can be sown in the open from early spring till early autumn and earlier or later than this in favourable places that get very little frost. They can also be sown in mid-winter in heated glasshouses or frames or in cold frames or cloches in late winter to early spring.

General cultivation Hoe between rows, otherwise hand-weed. Early sowings will need to be protected with mats or straw. Do not let them dry out, especially in frames. Because radishes develop quickly, little chemical weedkilling is needed apart from pre-sowing applications of paraquat/diquat to land which has been prepared for a week or so to allow weeds to germinate. Avoid really weedy ground for this crop.

Harvesting and storing Pull as required, preferably when young and tender. Will not store.

Plants per person 30   *Yield per plant* 28–42 g ($1-1\frac{1}{2}$ oz)

Pests and diseases Not greatly troubled by pests or diseases, though flea beetle can be a nuisance. Use Gamma-HCH dust when nicks are seen in leaves.

Varieties French Breakfast (most popular variety, olive shaped); Saxa, Cherry Belle (globe shaped); Rota (very good new radish, brilliant scarlet); Scarlet Globe (for forcing and outdoors, deep scarlet); Sparkler (red turnip variety); Long White Icicle (long tapering roots, good flavour); Black Spanish Long (winter use only, long black roots, white flesh); China Rose (winter use, long, roots bright rose).

RHUBARB

Hardy. This is one of the oldest plants in cultivation and long recognized for its medicinal properties. It is grown for its stalks, which are used as fruit for cooking and for jam making. There are two ways of growing rhubarb: outdoors throughout, and forcing roots in darkness to produce succulent blanched shoots.

Site and soil preparation Most soils will grow rhubarb, indeed it is often relegated to an out-of-the-way corner where soil is of doubtful quality. Best results come from good soil and deep digging, pH 5–6, soil index N:P:K 2–3. An open sunny situation, away from hedges or the overhang of buildings is ideal.

Before planting dig in farmyard manure at a heavy rate. After crop is established use a 12:5:6 fertilizer at 140 g per m² (4 oz per sq yd). Give this as growth commences in the early part of the year. It is specially important when producing crowns for forcing. Such lavish treatment is seldom given to garden rhubarb, but a little annual scattering of fertilizer never goes amiss.

Sowing and planting Seeds required: 1 small packet. Viability 70 per cent.

Rhubarb can be raised from seeds but is slow to develop. It may also vary from the type. Sow the seeds in mild heat in early spring and prick out the resultant seedlings 30 × 30 cm (12 × 12in) apart in a sheltered spot out of doors, where they remain until planted in their permanent position. The usual way to increase plants is by division. But for a good start it is best to buy in new crowns from a reliable source. Plant about 1 metre (1 yd) apart each way in well-prepared ground free from serious perennial weeds.. Plant with the spike-like crowns just *above* soil level. If below, they could rot.

General cultivation Apart from hoeing, rhubarb looks after itself fairly well. It is not advisable to pull any shoots the first year after planting unless the crowns were very large and vigorous. Remove any flower stalks which form. Lift the crowns every 5 – 6 years, detach the younger, outer portions with a sharp spade and replant these.

Chemical weedkilling is unlikely to be necessary in rhubarb grown on a small scale. For larger beds use dalapon (foliage-acting) during the dormant period against couch grass, simazine (soil-acting) during dormancy to weed-free soil.

Harvesting and storing Pull as required, taking care not to damage the centre of the crowns by pulling out the shoots roughly. Hold the stem low down and give a slight twist before pulling. Early stalks can be harvested in early spring by covering the crown with an inverted bucket or box in late winter. Will not store fresh, but young stems can be deep frozen. Good for bottling.

Forcing
There are various degrees of forcing rhubarb, ranging from putting a few boxes or large pots over selected crowns, placing a layer of straw over the plants, to (more effectively) lifting a few 3 – 4 year crowns in the early autumn and leaving them to get well frosted. (There is a cold unit technique for determining when the crowns have had enough cold, details of which are available in specialist publications). These roots are then

'Feltham First', one of the earliest cropping peas, is looked forward to as avidly as the first early potatoes.

trimmed to shape and placed in a dark cellar or shed or under a darkened bench in a greenhouse where, if watered regularly, they will produce blanched shoots at a rate varying with the temperature, which should ideally be around 13°C (55°F). Even a little light getting on to the shoots will cause them to colour and lose blanch and some succulence.

Plants per person 2 – 3   *Yield per plant* 2 – 4 kg (4–8 lb)

Pests and diseases Stem eelworm, crown gall, crown rot, grey mould, virus. Respond by buying new stock or planting on a new site.

Varieties Timperley Early, Hawkes Champagne, Prince Albert, Victoria and many more.

SHALLOTS
Hardy. A very useful and easy-to-grow vegetable producing bulbs similar in taste to onions but stronger.

Site and soil preparation See Onions.

Sowing and planting Shallots can be raised from seed in the same way as onions (1 small packet of seed; viability 70 per cent), but are generally bought as bulbs in the spring. Twist these bulbs gently into the soil 10–15 cm (4–6 in) apart, in rows 30 cm (1 ft) apart. Do this in late winter or early spring – shallots are one of the earliest vegetables to be started.

General cultivation Birds are a problem, especially until the shallots are firmly rooted. They will need protecting with thread or nets. Otherwise there is very little to do apart from hoeing and removing any flower heads.

Harvesting and storing In late summer when the foliage yellows ease the clumps out of the ground and let the bulbs ripen thoroughly in a sunny spot. Then split up the clumps ready to store in a cool dry place, as for onions. Can also be frozen.

Plants per person 8 – 10   *Yield per plant* 5 – 6 shallots

Pests and diseases None of consequence, but see Onion.

Varieties Red or yellow, oval or round forms available.

SPINACH
Half-hardy or hardy. Two well-known types of spinach are listed in

most seed catalogues – round, or summer spinach and the prickly winter type. There are also a number of closely allied plants which are grown like spinach, for their succulent, highly nutritious leaves. Perpetual spinach and seakale beet are dealt with under Beetroot. For Mountain and New Zealand spinach see following entries.

Site and soil preparation Any reasonable soil will grow spinach, apart from very light soils which dry out badly and invariably cause spinach to bolt. pH 6.5, soil index N:P:K 1–2. Any fairly good situation will do.

Deep digging and manuring with farmyard manure are desirable. Being a leaf crop spinach likes nitrogen, so a 12:8:8 fertilizer is required at 70g per m² (2 oz per sq yd). For winter spinach omit nitrogen.

Sowing and planting Seeds required: 28 g(1 oz) per 30 m (100 ft) row. Viability 60 per cent.

Spinach is grown for succession, being sown from late winter to early spring onwards at 2 – 3 week intervals in drills 2.5 cm (1 in) deep and 30 cm (1 ft) apart. It is essential to tread the soil firm and provide a good tilth before sowing. Thin seedlings to 15–22 cm (6–9 in) apart. Sow round types until late summer, then winter types about early autumn, thinning them less severely, to 11–15 cm (4–6 in) apart.

General cultivation This is a crop which must grow quickly and never dry out, or it will run to seed. Hoe between rows regularly, water if need be and if the weather is very dry mulch with peat, spent hops or other organic material. When weather is very dry water the ground before sowing the seeds, which should be soaked in water for 10–12 hours beforehand. An ideal crop for growing with cloche protection both early and late in the season.

Few weedkillers are satisfactory for spinach, which is susceptible to chemicals and is quick-maturing anyway. Preparing the bed a week or two before sowing and using paraquat/diquat before sowing is the simplest course.

Harvesting and storing Pull when required, largest leaves first. Distribute picking over plants in the row. Do not pick stems. If leaves do not break off readily, cut them off. Stores only in the freezer but is excellent for that.

Plants per person 5   *Yield per plant* Very variable,
                                             about 230 g (8 oz)

Pests and diseases Blackfly, leaf miner, downy mildew, leaf spot, spinach blight. Use a range of sprays if any of these are specially troublesome.

Varieties Greenmarket, Viking, Noorman.

SPINACH, *New Zealand*
Half-hardy. This has the virtue of not running to seed in dry seasons like ordinary spinach. It can be sown in gentle heat in early spring for planting outside in late spring at 60 cm (2 ft) in rows 90 cm (3 ft) apart, or sown direct in clumps from early spring until mid-spring in rows 90 cm (3 ft) apart, thinning to 60 cm (2 ft). It is grown like ordinary spinach except that it needs lighter soil.

SWEET CORN
Tender. This is very popular with gardeners who have the shelter needed to grow this crop to perfection. It is not a plant for exposed sites.

Site and soil preparation Medium to light soil, pH 6–6.5, soil index N:P:K 2–3. A sheltered and sunny situation is essential.

Cultivate the soil 30 cm (1 ft) deep. A firm bed is desirable, *not* loose puffy soil. Sweet corn is a leafy crop that likes nitrogen, so apply a 12:6:6 fertilizer at 70 g per m² (2 oz per sq yd) before sowing. Organic manure is best applied to the *previous* crop.

Sowing and planting Seeds required: 110 g (4 oz) per 30 m (100 ft). Viability 70 per cent.

Sweet corn can be sown in peat pots under glass in mid-spring for planting out at 30 × 60 cm (12 × 24 in) in late spring, which is the best procedure in cold areas. Alternatively, sow direct in mid to late spring spacing the seeds 22–30 cm (9–12 in) apart in rows 60 cm (2 ft) apart. It is better for pollination to plant in a square block rather than a long single row. Seeds sown outdoors, 2 or 3 per station are best covered with a cloche or with jam jars.

General cultivation Hoeing and watering are the two main requirements. Some shelter from cold winds with a plastic windbreak or even some old sacks will help this tender crop to get established. Some support may be required, especially in windy areas. Pollination is helped by gentle shaking.

Simazine weedkiller is recommended when this crop is grown on a large scale. But on a small scale hoeing should take care of all the weeds.

Harvesting and storing Cobs are ripe and ready for harvesting when the

If space is limited, rhubarb can be forced into early growth in a black polythene sack to yield succulent pink sticks.

little silks which protrude from the end of the cob begin to wither. Test one or two of the grains by pulling back the protective sheath and pressing with your finger and thumb to see if 'milk' is present. The cobs are a real delicacy for the table. Will not store fresh. Suitable for deep freezing.
Plants per person 10 − 12   *Yield per plant* 2 − 3 cobs

Pests and diseases Apart from earwigs which get into the cobs but do little harm, there are generally no real problems with this crop.

Varieties North Star, Vanguard (early American); John Innes Hybrid, Kelvedon Glory (English).

TOMATOES, OUTDOOR

For Indoor Tomatoes, see *Simple Tomato Growing* by Ian G Walls (Concorde)
Tender. Tomatoes are one of our most valuable salad foods. Their success outdoors depends almost entirely on weather and latitude. Most southern regions of the UK are ideal for outdoor culture, given a good season, but in many regions results can be good with protection at the beginning and the end of the season. Two types of tomato are grown: the excellent big, meaty tomato which is a favourite in the warmer lands of Europe and America, and the smaller round tomato still favoured in Britain.

Site and soil preparation Medium soil of good texture and high fertility, well-drained, pH 6.5, soil index N:P:K 3–4.

Select a site which affords protection from wind and receives the maximum amount of sun. A south-facing border in front of a high wall is ideal. Portable shelter materials can often be used to good effect, especially in the North.

Outdoor tomatoes are a short-term crop, so the total nutrient uptake is much less than for the longer season greenhouse crop. Deep digging is essential to improve drainage. Well-rotted farmyard manure, peat or compost should be given in sufficient quantities to improve soil texture – in the region of 10 kg per m² (20 lb per sq yd). Peat can be used instead of farmyard manure, but lime must also be applied to counteract the acidity of the peat.

Raised beds are often used for tomatoes, using ridges of John Innes No 2 Potting or soilless type compost, at roughly half a bushel (0.1m³) per plant, on top of polythene sheeting where pests or diseases are suspected in the soil. Growing in polythene-lined trenches filled with soilless compost can also be worth considering, provided drainage is not restricted. In recent years bolsters or growing bags as used in greenhouses have become very popular for outdoor culture but the economics of this system require close scrutiny.

Where special composts are *not* used, give an evenly spread base feed 10:10:20 at 140 g per m² (4 oz per sq yd) and rake well in, bringing the soil to a fine state for planting, i.e. fairly firm, yet with a good tilth on the surface.

Sowing and planting Seeds required: 1 small packet. Viability 75 per cent.

As tomatoes are tender, outdoor varieties are unlikely to be planted until around late spring in the South (perhaps a little earlier in the Channel Islands) and early summer in the North. To allow 5–6 weeks for raising the plants, the seeds need to be sown in mid-spring in mild heat.

Sow in 10 cm (4 in) pots or in large soil blocks, in John Innes Seed Compost or a soilless equivalent, and grow until the first truss is in flower in a cool greenhouse or raised open frame. Harden off well before planting out. If cloches are to be used to start the crop off out of doors, put them in position 10–14 days before planting to warm up the soil. This can advance planting by 2–3 weeks, especially in exposed areas.

Plant tomatoes about 38–45 cm (15–18 in) apart in rows 76–90 cm (30–36 in) apart. If there are several rows, run them north-south, but east-west where only a few rows are planted, especially if these are in south-facing borders.

General cultivation Suitably hardened off plants that have not become pot-bound should establish fairly rapidly. A light watering or spraying with clean water in hot weather helps them to establish. Stake them (except for bush varieties) immediately after planting with 1.5 m (5 ft) canes and secure with soft twine or paper and wire clips. Remove any cloches that have been used when the plants have developed sufficiently, and stake and tie the plants. They often appreciate some temporary shelter with old sacks. Plants tend to go a darker green outdoors than in a greenhouse due to the lower temperatures, and the foliage can become hard and curled as a result of the fluctuating day and night temperatures.

Once plants are established, feed them every 10–14 days, using a liquid feed high in potash. Adjust balance of feed according to rate of growth, giving more nitrogen if plants are too hard and more potash if too soft.

Continue tying in the tomato plants as they grow. Remove side shoots as for indoor tomatoes (except for bush varieties), and pinch out the tops of the plants above the third to fifth truss, according to the district and the likely length of season. If growth is slow, as it can be in a cool summer, it may only be possible to ripen two or three trusses.

Never allow the plants to dry out. A mulch of straw or peat will help conserve moisture. Spraying overhead with a hosepipe in dry weather helps set the fruit.

In early autumn put down a mulch of straw, sever the plants from their stakes and lay them down under cloches or polythene tunnels to encourage green fruits to ripen.

Where cloches are large enough – several tall designs are available – the plants can be grown under them right through the season. Training systems vary, but one suggestion is to run a wire horizontally on stakes 10 cm (4 in) beneath the top of the cloche and secure the plants to this. Much higher yields can be obtained under cloches. Some defoliation will definitely be necessary, removing the lower leaves as in a greenhouse. Bush varieties lend themselves admirably to being grown under cloches the whole season, though they must be regularly watered. It helps if trusses are supported on a low-set wire or on wire netting raised a little above ground level. They may need shading with a proprietary shading material, or lime and water, in very hot weather.

Harvesting and storing Pick when ripe. Ripen off the residue of the crop on windowsills, or between layers of straw in a completely darkened box in a temperature of 15–18°C (60–65°F). Green tomatoes make good chutney. Ripe fruits can be frozen whole or as purée or bottled.

Plants per person 4–6   *Yield per plant* Varies according to weather 1–1¼ kg (2–3 lb)

Bush tomatoes need no staking or de-shooting yet they yield prolific crops of smallish fruits.

Pests and diseases On a new site or using growing bags, soilborne troubles should not be a problem. Sucking and biting pests can be troublesome, so use insecticides regularly; Botrytis, which damages the leaves and fruits, and blight (blackens the leaves) could also appear. Spray with general copper-based fungicides – against blight. Many varieties are resilient to many of these troubles and these should be grown (see *Simple Tomato Growing*, Ian Walls, for full account of pests, diseases and troubles).

Varieties Outdoor varieties: Alfresco (vigorous, compact bushy plant); Sigmabush (F1 hybrid; outstanding for quality, earliness and yield; ripens even in poor conditions); French Cross (F1 hybrid; only from Suttons. One of the highest yielding of the bush varieties; well flavoured); Pixie Hybrid (ideal for large pots or containers on a patio or in other sunny position); The Amateur (popular variety, medium-sized fruits); Roma (Continental-type bearing long, brightly coloured, fleshy fruits. Heavy cropping, resistant to fusarium wilt).
Straight varieties (non-hybrid): Ailsa Craig-Leader (Suttons; quick matur-

ing, with small/medium, thin-skinned, fleshy fruits); Alicante (Suttons; a particularly popular variety, maturing early); Best of All (Suttons; large, very fleshy fruits with few seeds); Harbinger (Suttons. Crops well and ripens early); Moneymaker and Moneymaker Money Cross (the most popular variety in cultivation; heavy crops of medium-sized fruits); Ailsa Craig (medium-sized fruits of good flavour); Marmande (Continental outdoor variety; large irregular fruits); Golden Sunrise (medium-sized yellow fruits of distinctive flavour); Tangella (medium-sized, pale orange fruits of good flavour; ripens early).

Unusual tomatoes: Gardener's Delight; Sweet 100; Tiny Tim; Totem (F1 hybrid; grow in pots or windowboxes).

TURNIPS AND SWEDES

Half-hardy/hardy. Turnips are a most useful crop, ranging from the early salad types to the swede or Swedish turnip, one of the most dependable of winter vegetables as it can remain outside in the garden, even in a hard winter, until required.

Site and soil preparation Most soils will grow turnips, but early types grow best in rich fertile soil, whereas excellent swedes can be grown in

Well-grown turnips, like 'Snowball', which have not yet been allowed to become dry and woody, make a flavoursome addition to summer dishes.

'hungry' land. pH 6.5–7, soil index N:P:K 2. Use any reasonable situation.

Normal deep cultivation is all that is required. Fresh farmyard manure is not desirable, as it tends to induce forking and coarse roots. A firm bed is preferable. On sticky, heavy land, grow swedes on top of ridges. Before sowing give a 12:12:12 fertilizer at 70 g per m² (2 oz per sq yd), preferably concentrated along and beside the drills.

Sowing and planting Seeds required: 14 g ($\frac{1}{2}$ oz) per 30 m (100 ft) row. Viability 80 per cent.

The early crop can be sown in mild heat in a greenhouse or frame from mid-winter onwards, and in early to mid-spring in the open. In a greenhouse or frame sow in drills 1.5 cm ($\frac{1}{2}$ in) deep and 10–12 cm (4–6 in) apart. Outside, sow in drills 30 cm (1 ft) apart. Thin seedlings to 8–10 cm (3–4 in) apart. Swede rows should be at least 45 cm (18 in) apart. Thin seedlings to 20–30 cm (8–12 in) apart to keep roots small and tasty rather than large and coarse.

Sow thinly, as turnips germinate very well. Do not sow early or the seedlings could be frosted, a check which will cause them, particularly swedes, to run to seed.

General cultivation Apart from thinning and regular hoeing, this is an easy crop to manage. Weedkillers are unnecessary when growing on a small scale.

Harvesting and storing Pull when ready, using the salad types when very young and leaving the swedes in the ground. Cut off tops after lifting. Store, if necessary, in boxes of sand in a shed or in a properly made clamp outside. Freeze young turnips whole. Older ones and swedes should be cooked and mashed.

Plants per person 10–12   *Yield per plant* $\frac{1}{2}$–1 kg (1$\frac{1}{2}$–2$\frac{1}{2}$ lb)

Pests and diseases Watch particularly for clubroot and flea beetle. See also Brassica pests.

Varieties White Milan (early, quick-maturing); Purpletop Milan (early, flattish roots); Snowball (early, globe); Golden Ball (autumn, yellow-fleshed globe); Green Globe (winter use); Green Top Stone (spring or autumn, very small top); Manchester Market (white fleshed, good flavour); Best of All, Purple Top (medium sized swede, keeps well); Conqueror, Green Top (mild flavoured swede); Victory (purple-topped swede).